Chinese Students in America: Policies, Issues, and Numbers

Leo A. Orleans
for
The Committee on Scholarly Communication
with the People's Republic of China

NATIONAL ACADEMY PRESS
Washington, D.C. 1988

National Academy Press • 2101 Constitution Avenue, N.W. • Washington. D. C. 20418

NOTICE: The project that is the subject of this report was sponsored by the Committeee on Scholarly Communication with the People's Republic of China. The accuracy of the information presented and the views expressed in this publication are the responsibility of the author and not the sponsoring organization.

This study was made possible by funds provided by the Bureau of Educational and Cultural Affairs of the United States Information Agency under the authority of the Fulbright–Hays Act of 1961.

The Committee on Scholarly Communication with the People's Republic of China (CSCPRC) is jointly sponsored by the American Council of Learned Societies, the Social Science Research Council, and the National Academy of Sciences. The Academy provides an administrative base for the CSCPRC.

Since the normalization of diplomatic relations between the United States and China in 1979, the CSCPRC has developed programs with the Chinese Academy of Sciences (CAS), the Chinese Academy of Social Sciences (CASS), and the State Education Commission, in addition to those with the China Association for Science and Technology (CAST), with whom CSCPRC began exchanges in 1972. Current activities include a program for American graduate students and postdoctoral scholars to carry out long-term study or research in affiliation with Chinese universities and research institutes; a short-term reciprocal exchange of senior-level Chinese and American scholars; a bilateral conference program; and an exchange of joint working groups in selected fields.

CSCPRC programs are funded by the National Science Foundation, the U.S. Information Agency, the National Endowment for the Humanities, the U.S. Department of Education, the Ford Foundation, the Henry Luce Foundation, the John D. and Catherine T. MacArthur Foundation, the Andrew W. Mellon Foundation, the Rockefeller Foundation, the Starr Foundation, and select corporations.

Library of Congress Cataloging-in-Publication Data

Orleans, Leo A. Chinese students in America.

Bibliography: p. Includes index. 1.Chinese students—United States. I. Committee on Scholarly Communications with the People's Republic of China (U.S.) II. Title.
LC3071.074   1988   371.8'.2   88-22492 ISBN 0-309-03886-3

Printed in the United States of America

First Printing, September 1988
Second Printing, January 1989

Preface

Neither the Chinese nor the Americans know precisely how many Chinese students and scholars are in the United States now or at any time since exchanges began in 1978. Yet, numerous government agencies, universities, and other institutions in the United States that interact with the Chinese through a variety of exchange agreements and cooperative research projects are anxious to have more information about the students and scholars in this country, their numbers, and their characteristics.

This need inspired an earlier effort by the Committee on Scholarly Communication with the People's Republic of China (CSCPRC), with the support of the U.S. Information Agency (USIA) and the Ford Foundation, to undertake a study of Chinese students and scholars in the United States, set in the context of a more general look at the development of the extensive academic exchange programs that have evolved between the two countries. This effort produced a groundbreaking study by David M. Lampton (with Joyce A. Mandancy and Kristen M. Williams), entitled *A Relationship Restored: Trends in U.S.–China Educational Exchanges, 1978–1984*, published by the National Academy Press in 1986.

Although this current study, *Chinese Students in America: Policies, Issues, and Numbers,* is also sponsored by the CSCPRC and supported by the USIA, it approaches educational exchanges with

iii

the People's Republic of China from a somewhat different perspective. Part I looks at China's evolving policies with regard to sending students and scholars abroad for study and Beijing's concerns and efforts to obtain maximum return from this expensive and somewhat risky enterprise. Although interspersed with commentary and opinions, Part I is based almost exclusively on Chinese articles, documents, and pronouncements on the subject. This first part, then, differs from the Lampton study, which looked at the U.S.–China academic exchanges essentially from the U.S. perspective.

Part II of this report analyzes statistics on the flow of Chinese students and visiting scholars entering and leaving the United States since 1979, their fields of specialization, sources of funding, and a variety of personal characteristics. It updates the Lampton study, adding two to three years to the basic statistics, and I am entirely indebted to David Lampton and his colleagues for the procedures and methodologies they developed to handle the quantitative data on which both studies rely. The statistical analysis is based on two types of material: (1) visa data submitted to U.S. embassy and consular offices in the People's Republic of China, the input of a laborious task of manually coding the information in each visa application, and (2) USIA data tapes containing all the IAP-66 forms, which are filled out annually by U.S. institutions of higher education for students and scholars who receive J-1 visas. Some comparisons are also made between U.S. and Chinese statistics, and an effort is made to estimate the number of Chinese students and scholars in the United States and the number who had returned home.

Although this study is divided into two distinct parts, there is, of course, an obvious and intimate relationship between Beijing's evolving policies with regard to foreign study, the number of individuals who manage to come to the United States for study and research, and the qualifications and characteristics of the students and scholars.

Every study owes "special thanks" to someone. In this instance they go to Mary B. Bullock, who saw the need for this study, obtained the necessary support, and succeeded in transferring her enthusiasm to the author.

Kristen Williams provided the computer expertise in handling and analyzing the statistics, and her experience in working on the earlier study made for invaluable continuity. Joyce Madancy spent a long summer in China performing the unenviable task of translating the information from the visa applications to a machine-readable code.

This study was done in spurts and pauses over a protracted period of time, so that more than the usual number of friends and colleagues (volunteers and conscripts) have had a chance to comment on the manuscript as it went through various revisions and expansions. First, my sincere appreciation to George Beckmann, Andrea Gay, Ruth Hayhoe, Todd Johnson, Victor Rabinowitch, Kyna Rubin, and Mitchel Wallerstein for their useful comments and suggestions. And second, an exalted level of appreciation to Mary B. Bullock, David M. Lampton, Douglas P. Murray, Michel C. Oksenberg, Glenn Shive, and Richard P. Suttmeier, who went beyond the call of duty to provide me with most careful and thorough readings and critiques, which would both delight and frustrate any author. While I am grateful to all for their time and effort, they will undoubtedly be relieved to know that all the responsibility for the contents of this book rests with me alone.

Being accepted as part of the CSCPRC family was a privilege, and I greatly appreciate the friendship and good will of everyone on the staff (including those who have gone on to other adventures). I especially want to thank Terry Price and Jennifer Hess for holding my hand as I advanced from kindergarten to middle school in word processing, to Kathlin Smith for feeding me some interesting tidbits I might have otherwise missed, and, of course, to the most able and always helpful Alice Bishop for everything.

At the National Academy Press, I wish to express my appreciation to Heather Wiley for her expert copyediting of the manuscript, to Jim Gormley for managing the art production, and to Sally Fields, who, with gentle proficiency, managed the difficult process of pulling the various pieces together into the final publication.

My good friend Chi Wang suggested the Chinese characters on the cover and kindly did the calligraphy. Together, the characters *liu* and *xue* mean, quite appropriately, "study abroad."

Finally, I would like to take this opportunity to thank Dorothy Clark not only for her "author-friendly" editing of an early draft of this manuscript but also for her unacknowledged contributions on scores of other manuscripts.

LEO A. ORLEANS
June 1988

Contents

Introduction   1

Part I
CHINA'S POLICIES AND PROBLEMS

1   The Evolving Policies   19
    Background—The First Three Decades, 19
    Resuming the Exchanges, 22
    Experience and Change, 25
    Problems of Implementation, 33

2   The Brain-Drain Issue   36
    Government-Sponsored Students and Scholars, 38
    Privately Sponsored Students, 39
    The Students' Perspective, 42
    Prospects, 49
    The International Perspective, 53

3   Problems in Utilizing Returning Students and Scholars   57
    China's System of Job Assignments and
    Job Mobility, 59
    The Mounting Problems, 61
    The Legitimacy of the Complaints, 65
    Some Proposed Solutions, 68

Part II
CHINESE STUDENTS AND SCHOLARS
IN THE UNITED STATES:
NUMBERS AND CHARACTERISTICS

4   Understanding the Statistics: Problems and Issues   77
        Chinese Statistics on Sending Students Abroad, 77
        U.S. Immigration and Naturalization Service
        Data on Chinese Students, 82
        Statistics from Visa Applications and USIA Data Tapes, 84

5   Statistics on Trends and Characteristics of Exchange
    Participants from China   87
        J-1 and F-1 Students and Scholars, 88
        J-1 and F-1 Students, 94
        J-1 Visiting Scholars, 106
        Estimating the Number of Students and Scholars
        in the United States, 109

Conclusion: Chinese Students: An Emerging Issue in
             U.S.–China Relations?   114

APPENDIX   State Education Commission Provisions on Study
           Abroad   123

Index   139

Introduction

It is unfortunate that between the initiation and conclusion of this study, the relatively routine process of sending Chinese students and scholars to the United States has moved from governmental and institutional concerns to the front pages of newspapers both here and in China.* In the course of some 18 months the subject of Chinese students abroad has become much more conducive to short op-ed pieces than to monographs, and the spring of 1988 has become an especially unpropitious time to set down any concrete conclusions regarding Chinese students and scholars in U.S. institutions of higher education. It is therefore useful to go back a couple of years and run through some of the developments in China that may have had a bearing on the policy of sending students and scholars abroad, and on the attitudes and concerns of students who are already abroad.

In December 1986 and January 1987, the world was once again startled by the news from China of student demonstrations, the expulsion of some highly placed intellectuals from their posts, the dismissal of Hu Yaobang as General Secretary of the Communist Party, and what, at that time, appeared to be a victory for the "conservative" elements in the leadership. The general concern about the

---

*In this study, the terms China and People's Republic of China (PRC) are used interchangeably.

1

possible effects of these actions on China's domestic reforms and on her policy of opening to the world was quickly translated into a more parochial worry: what effect will these changes have on the policy of sending scholars abroad—especially to the United States, where "bourgeois democracy" flourishes? And how badly was the foreign study program aggravated by the vocal support of many Chinese students already in the United States—as expressed, for example, in an open letter in the *New York Times*[1] signed by some 1,000 Chinese studying in the United States, expressing concern about the dismissal of Hu Yaobang, the punishment and criticism of some prominent intellectuals, and the "ultra-leftist" practice of labeling people arbitrarily? After all, unlike the short-lived 1983 campaign against "spiritual pollution" (the absorption of foreign ideas and life-styles through exposure to foreign printed and visual materials and contact with foreigners living in or visiting the country), this time the problem was much more serious than jeans and haircuts and the "worshiping of foreign things."

The new demands of the students, especially of their outspoken leaders, were for freedom, democracy, and human rights and could be interpreted as blatant attacks on Communist ideology and the system. For example, Fang Lizhi, the fired Vice-President of the University of Science and Technology in Hefei (Anhui Province) and one of the most outspoken advocates of more independent thinking, was adamant in his criticism of the "undemocratic practices in the society" and the "doctrine of obedience" practiced by his colleagues, proclaiming that democracy embodies the recognition of individual rights.[2] Other critics were only slightly more discreet, couching their demands in more appropriate language. Yang Xinguan, for example, asked why China has no problem with the importation of modern science, technology, and management techniques from advanced countries, but refuses to import and absorb new ideologies, concepts, and methodologies, which are so closely linked with the development of the advanced nations. China should not be afraid of new ideas, said Yang, because "Marxists are fearless."[3]

---

[1] *New York Times*, Jan. 23, 1986.

[2] *Shijie Jingji Daobao* (*World Economic Herald*), Nov. 24, 1986; Foreign Broadcast Information Service (hereafter referred to as FBIS), Dec. 19, 1986, p. K13.

[3] Yang Xinguang, "Cultural Imports and Exchanges in the Course of Opening Up to the Outside World," *Guangming Ribao* (hereafter referred to as *GMRB*), June 7, 1986; translated in Joint Publications Research Service (hereafter referred to as JPRS), CPS-86-060, July 25, 1986, p. 4.

Understandably, articles and speeches by some of the more vocal proponents of "democracy" worried other intellectuals who feared that, coupled with the student demonstrations, they were bound to "kill the golden goose." And indeed, Beijing must have felt that freedom of speech, limited as it was to a minute segment of the population, had gone too far. Not to respond to such attacks would not only encourage "bourgeois liberalization" but might also be interpreted as a sign of weakness. However, the subsequent crackdown on intellectual dissent was mild by any standard and essentially limited to highly placed individuals. As for the demonstrating students, officials first excused these activities by pointing out that, according to the PRC Constitution, "Chinese citizens have the right to hold demonstrations" and that student concerns were "understandable," while, for foreign consumption, insisting that the demonstrations had more to do with complaints about student housing and food than with politics. As the marches continued, however, the call went out for greater student restraint and the use of "normal democratic channels." Some students expressed the view that one of the compelling reasons for China's quick decision to calm domestic concerns and to use relatively gentle means in reprimanding the dissidents was an awareness of the adverse effects stronger measures might have had on students and scholars who were abroad.[4]

The pacification campaign initiated by the Communist Party after the disturbances was directed primarily at two groups most sensitive to any policy changes: foreign investors and Chinese intellectuals. Foreign investors were assured that the policy against "bourgeois liberalization" did not contradict the policy of opening to the outside world, that the number of contracts signed and money invested will continue to increase, and that foreign investors who take a wait-and-see attitude will lose out in the long run.[5] As for the intellectuals, trusted scholars and respected officials were enlisted to

---

[4] Some students also maintained that it was their demonstrations for democracy that spurred Zhao Ziyang, the then General Secretary of the Communist Party of China (CPC), to call for political reforms in his October 25, 1987 report to the Thirteenth Party Congress. In the words of one student, "Our ideas were abstract and we wanted things too quickly, but the student movement had a definite effect on the whole society" (Nina McPherson, "Students Say Protests Effective," Hong Kong AFP, Oct. 30, 1987; FBIS-Chi-87-210, Oct. 30, 1987, p. 21).

[5] See, for example, press interview of State Councilor Gu Mu, in *Wen Wei Po* (Hong Kong), April 2, 1987; translated in FBIS, April 2, 1987, p. K5.

make assurances that the fight against "bourgeois liberalization" was not aimed at them. Special attention was accorded the scientific and technical personnel, who were told that "we must never label rashly the different views and understanding over academic problems of natural science as advocating bourgeois liberalization."[6] Occasional warnings that capitalist countries are no "paradise on earth" and that "Western bourgeois democracy is not a flower"[7] were lost in the flood of assurances that "the struggle against bourgeois liberalization will be strictly confined within the Chinese Communist Party and conducted chiefly in the political-ideological domain. . . ."[8] General Secretary Zhao Ziyang assured Secretary of State George Shultz that "the question of altering reforms and the policy of opening to the outside world does not exist,"[9] while Deng Xiaoping went even further when he said that, if there are any shortcomings in China's opening to the outside world, "they are chiefly manifested in the fact [that] the door has not been opened wide enough."[10]

Although foreign apprehension continued to be fed by quotations attributed to innumerable unidentified "observers" who were citing a conservative victory and, some wishfully and some apprehensively, warning that "Maoist winds are howling with a vengeance" in China, by late 1987 it seemed clear that China was not backtracking either with regard to economic reforms or to the opening to the outside world. In hindsight, however, we know that 1987 was indeed a pivotal year with regard to students studying in the United States. Until then, Beijing had grudgingly accepted the fact that a large proportion of privately sponsored students with F-1 visas would not return, but seemed confident that the government-sponsored students and scholars with J-1 visas would be coming home on completion of their studies (see Glossary, pp. 6 and 7). In 1987 the concern began to grow that an ever-larger proportion of J-1 visa holders might also be looking for ways to remain in the United States, or at least to postpone their return. What were some of the reasons for this perceived change in the attitude of the students?

There is no doubt that the student demonstrations and the

---

[6] *China Daily* (hereafter referred to as *CD*), Feb. 28, 1987, p. 1.

[7] See, for example, Xinhua, Dec. 26, 1986; FBIS, Jan. 6, 1987, p. K2.

[8] Xinhua, April 11, 1987; FBIS, April 14, 1987, p. K19.

[9] *CD*, March 3, 1987, p. 1.

[10] Zhongguo Xinwen She (China News Agency, Hong Kong), Jan. 20, 1987; FBIS, Jan. 20, 1987, p. K5.

dismissals of some academic spokesmen for democracy and freedom of speech visibly alarmed the Chinese student community abroad, albeit the developments at home may have simply provided a timely excuse and a nudge for decisions that were already made or in the process of being made. By 1987 large numbers of students who came to the United States in the early 1980s were completing their degree programs and approaching their scheduled return. At the same time, the initial timidity of Chinese students who had lived in this country for a number of years disappeared. Through personal experience and word of mouth, they had "learned the ropes" and had become much wiser about U.S. customs and laws, discovering that unless one commits a crime, neither the Immigration and Naturalization Service nor any other branch of the U.S. government is likely to search them out for deportation.

In 1987 it became much more common for students to voice their desire to postpone the return decision until they were personally assured that conditions at home were nonthreatening and, more important, that if they returned, they would be working in prestigious institutions and within their specialties—conditions that China admittedly has difficulty in meeting. Others, apparently, do not hesitate in expressing their desire to remain in the United States—a fairly common impression among professors and college administrators who have routine professional contact with Chinese students.

It is not uncommon for Chinese officials to lament the growing tendency among their students to be much more self-centered, more aggressive in the pursuit of their professional goals, and to show much less concern about how their decisions may reflect on their country. And looking on from the outside, one could also conclude that once again China has been unable to find the elusive "happy medium" between Mao's "serve the people" and today's "it is alright to be rich" slogans. In one decade, and no doubt as an understandable reaction to the Cultural Revolution, the country went from a *mood* of altruism to a *mood* of selfishness. Clearly, many of the students now abroad are missing the ideological underpinnings that might have inculcated in them a sense of obligation to return home.

How will these attitudes on the part of students and concerns on the part of Beijing affect the future of sending students abroad? Ever in a state of flux, China's policies are constantly "adjusted" to reflect the nation's current needs and concerns. And because there is a significant gap between policies and implementation, each new directive and regulation spawns new rumors on the part of students

DEFINITIONS

F-1 VISA   The type of visa issued to foreign citizens who want to study in the United States at any level of school from precollege to graduate study. To qualify, a person must receive an I-20 form from an American institution that shows that they intend to pursue a full course of study in a field for which they qualify. Students with F-1 visas have usually developed their plan to study on their own or with the help of overseas relatives.

F-2 VISA   The type of visa issued to family members of a person holding an F-1 visa.

I-20   A form issued to applicants for F-1 visas, which documents that they have been accepted into a program offering a full course of study. This form is issued by the school administering the program and must be presented when applying for an F-1 visa.

IAP-66   A form issued to applicants for J-1 visas, which documents that they qualify under one of the programs designated by the United States Information Agency (USIA). This form is issued by the school or other institution, such as a hospital, and must be presented when applying for a J-1 visa.

J-1 VISA   The type of visa issued to persons who qualify under a program designated by USIA. Unlike the F-1 visas, the J-1 visas are not issued only to students, but also to several other categories of visitors, including research scholars, teachers, trainees, and international visitors. Most persons who are sponsored by the PRC government receive J-1 visas, which denote a higher level of scholarship than the F-1 visas. To receive a J-1 visa, an applicant must possess a valid IAP-66 form and is generally subject to the "two-year rule" (see below).

OFFICIALLY SPONSORED   Refers to those PRC students and scholars who have been chosen to come to the United States by the Chinese government and/or subordinate organizations. Most J-1 visa holders are officially sponsored, but some are not. And while most F-1 visa holders are *not* officially sponsored, there are also a few exceptions. Official sponsorship does not necessarily mean that the Chinese government is paying the expenses of the student or scholar; many of them have fellowships and scholarships from American sources.

RESEARCH OR VISITING SCHOLAR A category of J-1 visa holder who comes to the United States to study and do research but who does not enroll in a degree program. Research or visiting scholars may go to research institutions rather than to universities. They tend to be older than "students."

SELF-SUPPORTING Students and scholars who come to the United States from China without being chosen by the Chinese government. They are most commonly F-1 visa holders, although some J-1 students and scholars have also made their own arrangements. The money for their support usually comes from overseas relatives, although they also may qualify for scholarships and fellowships from American institutions.

TWO-YEAR RULE An American legal regulation that applies to some persons issued J-1 visas, which requires that the person reside outside of the United States for two years following the time in which they held a J-1 visa in the United States before they are eligible to apply for an immigrant visa or certain categories of nonimmigrant visas. The consular officer who issues the J-1 visa makes a determination at the time of visa issuance as to whether the person has received aid from the United States government or the Chinese government. If they have received such aid, they are subject to the two-year rule. Waivers to this rule can only be granted by USIA.

SOURCE: Adapted from David M. Lampton, *A Relationship Restored: Trends in U.S.-China Educational Exchanges, 1978–1984* (Washington, D.C.: National Academy Press, 1986), pp. 251–253.

who are now abroad and those who aspire to foreign education, as well as misinterpretations on the part of the news media and frustrations on the part of foreign-student advisers and professors in U.S. universities. The first half of 1988 was just such a period, with a rash of rumors about severe cuts in the number of Chinese who will be permitted to study in the United States, student petitions addressed to leaders in Beijing, denials by Chinese officials, and articles in newspapers and journals by U.S. reporters and observers. Despite rumor and confusion, there is no reason to question Beijing's assurances that the policy of sending scholars abroad—and specifically to the United States—will survive.

The Chinese may see foreign education as a source of undesired social change, but the knowledge and skills brought back by returning students are too important to sacrifice. Because there is no known immunization against "bourgeois liberalization," Beijing will be attempting to limit defection not by drastic cuts in overall numbers, but by changing the characteristics of the students sent abroad. Most will be PhD candidates or postdoctorate researchers, they will be somewhat older, they will have spent some time working at home before going abroad, most will be returning to the work unit they left, and their fields of study will be less theoretical and more closely reflect China's needs and the needs of their work unit. While Chinese Embassy and consular officials will have more precise responsibilities in overseeing their nationals, China will continue to be cautious in taking any actions that might be interpreted as coercive or in violation of human rights and personal freedoms. Such actions would not only affect the morale and effectiveness of those who return under duress, but cause an unwelcome public outcry in the United States.

The primary objectives of the visit of He Dongchang, Vice-Chairman of the State Education Commission, to the United States in June 1987 were, first, to assure U.S. institutions involved in educational exchanges with China that the process will continue uninterrupted; and second, to meet firsthand with U.S. officials and Chinese Embassy representatives to discuss what steps could be taken by all concerned to increase the likelihood that Chinese students will be coming home. Ideally, China would like to see the U.S. government take the lead in assuring the return of their nationals by implementing the existing immigration laws—pointing to the Western European nations and Japan as examples. The United States, however, is a nation of immigrants and has a very different attitude toward the desire of promising newcomers to remain in the country. It is therefore most unlikely that either the U.S. government or the universities would be willing or able to single out Chinese students for special surveillance and possible deportation.

At this juncture, no one can possibly predict how many of the Chinese students and scholars now in the United States will return and how many will manage to remain beyond the completion of their studies. It is well to remember, however, that even in the case of those who chose to remain, the defection may not be permanent. In the long run, and especially if the living and working conditions for intellectuals in China improve, the pull of family and country and/or the push of disillusionment with their prospects in the United States may induce many of the students and scholars to return home. This is not an unfamiliar pattern for students from other nations—especially in East Asia.

With the above perspective in mind, let us look at some of the specific study highlights.

• The sending of students and scholars abroad for degrees and research opportunities continues to be an integral part of China's policy to upgrade the educational system and provide the nation with the professional manpower necessary to meet the goals of modernization. From 1979 through 1987, the U.S. Department of State issued about 56,000 visas to visiting scholars and students from the People's Republic of China (Figure 1). About 60 percent of this total were selected by Chinese institutions for official sponsorship and came on J-1 visas, which have shown a steady annual increase between 1979 and 1987 (Figure 2). The remaining 40 percent were students with F-1 visas, who were privately supported by family and friends. As of this writing, and concerns about "bourgeois liberalization" notwithstanding, the flow of Chinese students to the United States and other countries has shown no sign of abatement and China contends that the policy will continue "in a planned way for a long time to come."

• It is estimated that in January 1988 there were approximately 21,000 Chinese scholars and students with J-1 visas and approximately 7,000 students with F-1 visas enrolled in degree programs or doing research in U.S. universities, for a total of 28,000. Since 1978, an additional 8,000 students, who came on F-1 visas, have managed to remain in this country, either by legally changing their status or simply disappearing into the American melting pot.

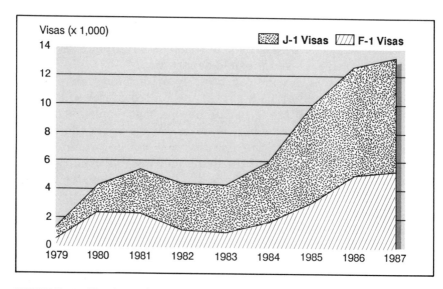

FIGURE 1 Number of J-1 and F-1 visas issued to PRC students and scholars, 1979–1987. SOURCE: From Table 5-1.

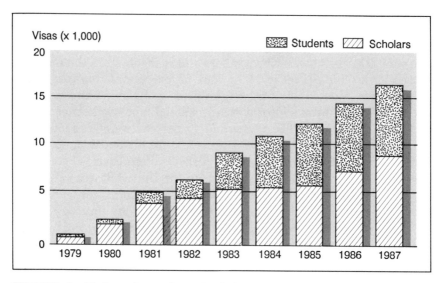

FIGURE 2 Estimated number of officially sponsored (J-1) students and scholars in the United States. SOURCE: From Table 5-27 and estimates in Chapter 5.

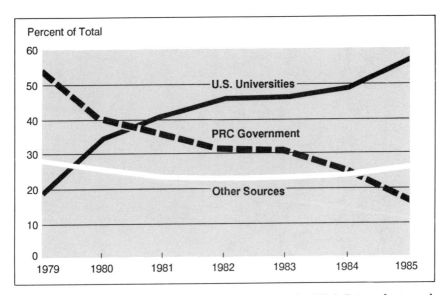

FIGURE 3 Changes in source of financial support for PRC J-1 students and scholars, 1979–1985. SOURCE: From Table 5-5.

- One of the most visible changes occurred in the sources of financial support. In 1979, 54 percent of the students and scholars with J-1 visas were supported by the Chinese government or by their work unit. By 1985, however, this proportion dropped to only 17 percent, while 57 percent of these academically competitive and highly motivated individuals managed to find funding from U.S. universities (Figure 3). The scholars' proportion of university funding is lower than that of students, because in 1985 approximately 10 percent of their support came from U.S. government agencies and foundations (7 and 3 percent, respectively).
- Reflecting China's priorities, engineering and science continue to be the dominant, but gradually diminishing, fields of specialization for both students and scholars with J-1 visas (Figure 4). Among the privately sponsored students (F-1 visas), a much higher proportion is enrolled in business management, computer sciences, and especially in the humanities (Figure 5). Both students and scholars are younger now than they were when the exchanges were initiated (Figure 6), but there has been little change in their places of origin, with the great majority continuing to come from the large urban centers of China's coastal provinces. In 1985 women constituted 20 percent of the J-1 students and 41 percent of the F-1 students.

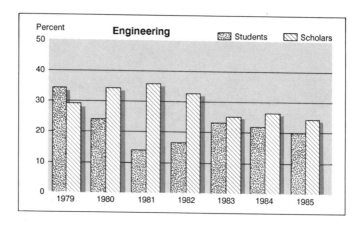

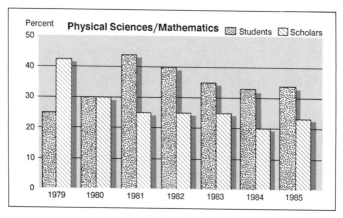

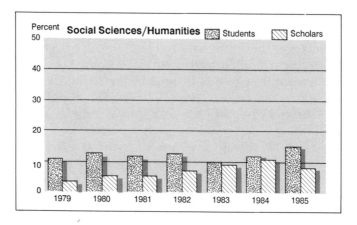

FIGURE 4   Distribution by field of study of PRC J-1 students and scholars entering new programs, 1979–1985. SOURCE: From Table 5-15.

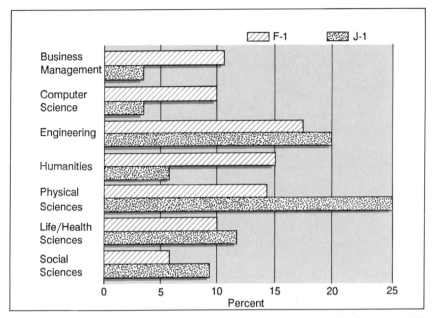

FIGURE 5   Distribution of PRC F-1 and J-1 students by field of study, 1985. SOURCE: From Tables 5-15 and 5-16.

- As China's own universities improved, expanded, and established graduate departments, the emphasis in foreign education shifted almost entirely to scholars and graduate students at the PhD and postdoctoral levels. China now projects 10,000 home-trained PhDs by the year 1990, who will then comprise the primary pool from which individuals will be selected for postdoctoral training and research abroad. As part of this change in priorities, Beijing intends that all graduate students (including those who find independent financing) go abroad only under official auspices and that they apply for J-1 visas, which have more definite limitations on length of stay in the United States. So far, this policy has not been reflected in a reduction of F-1 visas issued by the U.S. Embassy and Consulates in China.

- It is estimated that between 1978 and January 1988 approximately 12,500 J-1s and 7,000 F-1s returned to China, for a total of 19,500 returnees. At least prior to the student demonstrations in the winter of 1986–1987, virtually all the officially sponsored students and scholars returned to China after completing their programs. Those who decided to remain in this country were, for the most

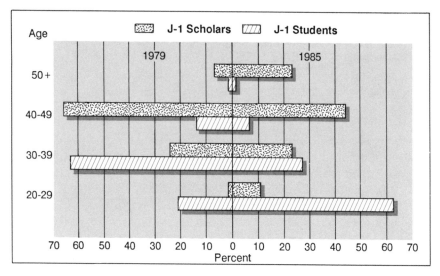

FIGURE 6   Distribution by age of PRC J-1 students and scholars entering new programs, 1979 and 1985. SOURCE: From Tables 5-10 and 5-23.

part, privately funded students. Thus, the concern expressed about the "brain-drain" issue in the mid-1980s was somewhat premature. Now, however, it appears that many of the students are taking a wait-and-see attitude and attempting at least to postpone their return to China.

• Some of the new measures introduced by Beijing to increase the likelihood that new students going abroad will return include: the shifting of the responsibility for selecting students for foreign education to individual work units; the introduction of signed contracts between the units and the individuals going abroad, stipulating the rights and responsibilities of each party—in some cases requiring a guarantor to financially promise their return; the provision that graduates of Chinese universities spend two years working before going abroad for advanced degrees; and, at the same time, the continuation of efforts to improve the living and working conditions at home for all intellectuals. It is important to keep in mind, however, that there is often a significant discrepancy between national policies and their implementation by local authorities. This is definitely the case with foreign-study regulations.

• Although there are still frequent complaints about the misuse of returning professionals, students and scholars who studied abroad tend to move up more rapidly within the administrative and research establishments. It is noteworthy that most of the complaints are identical to those expressed by graduates of Chinese universities and not altogether different from laments of scholars in other countries. Indeed, the misassignment of scholars returning from abroad is a real problem, but at the same time it is fair to suggest that many of the complaints expressed by the returnees are exaggerated and reflect unrealistic expectations. As the Chinese see it, one of the solutions to this problem is not simply utilizing what the students learned abroad, but making sure that what they learn is, in fact, what the country needs and is able to utilize. Consequently, while authorities hope to improve the job assignment process, they also stress the need for students to select specialties that will more closely match Chinese requirements and priorities and, while abroad, supplement their academic courses with as much practical experience as possible—especially within industrial enterprises.

PART I

China's Policies
and Problems

1
The Evolving Policies

BACKGROUND—THE FIRST THREE DECADES

During the past hundred years, and especially since the 1911 Revolution, China's more progressive leaders have strived to accelerate the country's modernization by sending students abroad to acquire both knowledge and know-how. And indeed, prior to 1949, students who completed their higher education in Japan, Europe, and the United States returned to China to play an important role in the awakening society.[1] They did this not only within their chosen professions, but also by bringing with them new political concepts and ideas and, in many instances, by assuming significant positions within the volatile governments in the first half of the twentieth century. Unfortunately, there were too many obstacles to be overcome and the modernization goals remained unfulfilled. For a country the size of China, the number of students was too small and too concentrated in the large coastal cities; internal politics and foreign wars inevitably interrupted and disrupted what steps may have been taken in modernizing the economy and the body politic; and, while seeking knowledge from abroad, the Chinese leaders (and, for that

---

[1] See, for example, Mary Brown Bullock, "American Exchanges with China Revisited," in Joyce K. Kallgren and Denis F. Simon, eds. *Educational Exchanges: Essays on the Sino-American Experience* (Berkeley: University of California, 1977).

matter, the populace in general) were never really comfortable with the gradual erosion of traditional Confucian patterns—ever modifying imported methods and substance to assure compatibility with traditional culture and to insure political control.

Not long after the creation of the new government in 1949, China once again turned to the outside to accelerate the process of training specialists—this time relying on her socialist neighbor to the north. Assistance from the Soviets in the 1950s went well beyond industrial plants and technology; they also helped with China's manpower needs by training over 10,000 people in Soviet universities and higher technical schools.[2] As in the case of Chinese students trained in other foreign countries, those trained in the Soviet Union also came back, gradually to assume key positions in the economy and the government of China. By 1956–1957, however, relations between Moscow and Beijing began to deteriorate, reached a critical period during the Great Leap Forward (1958–1959), and virtually broke down in 1960–1961. Moscow recalled all its specialists from China and, although a small number of Chinese students stayed on in the Soviet Union through the mid-1960s, for all practical purposes this was also the end of educational exchanges between the two countries—not to be resumed until the 1980s. As a postscript, it should be noted that in the case of the Soviet Union it would be surprising if a single Chinese student was lost to "brain drain."[3]

Disillusioned with the political costs of Soviet assistance, and despite limited economic relations with Japan and some of the Western European countries, in the 1960s Mao made China into a near-recluse country by embarking on a long period in which *self-sufficiency* and

---

[2] This general-use figure reported by Soviet sources and early Chinese publications has now been supplemented by more precise statistics published by the Chinese. According to Huang Shiqi, retired Director of the Information and Documentation Unit of the State Education Commission, between 1949 and 1966, China sent 8,424 students to the Soviet Union (only 206 after 1960) and 1,109 students to East European socialist countries. "About [*sic*] 7,324 students finished their studies in the Soviet Union" and 776 in Eastern Europe. According to Huang, the higher figures include "a significant number of trainees sent by industrial ministries and also a number of students sent by the Ministry of Defense." (Huang Shiqi, "Contemporary Educational Relations with the Industrialized World: A Chinese View" in Ruth Hayhoe and Marianne Bastid, eds. *China's Education and the Industrialized World* [Armonk, N.Y.: M. E. Sharpe, 1987], p. 225.)

[3] For a discussion of some of the factors behind this assertion, see Leo A. Orleans, "The 'Chinese Threat' and Soviet Emotions," *Russia*, No. 1 (1981), pp. 46–50.

self-reliance became the national bywords. With the exception of several thousand students who studied languages (primarily in the United Kingdom, France, Canada, West Germany, and Japan), no one from China went abroad for professional training during the 1960s and the first half of the 1970s.[4] According to one source, unique in the precision of the figure it cites, from 1950 through 1979 China sent 16,676 students to study abroad—a reasonable total.[5] Educational, scientific, and commercial contacts with the outside world were resumed in 1971–1972, but it was not until after Mao's death in 1976 that China, in her drive toward modernization, once again began to view foreign study as one of the shortcuts to the acquisition of world-level scientific and technical knowledge.

In the case of the United States, the primary motivation of President Nixon's 1972 visit to China and the rapprochement that followed had political and strategic roots; but these initial contacts were quickly followed by apolitical scholarly and scientific exchanges, which became the vital first strands in the cables of a bridge that would be built between the two countries in the years that followed. After the normalization of relations between the United States and the People's Republic of China in 1979, strategic considerations were quickly reinforced by a wide range of commercial, governmental, and institutional contacts.[6] The decision to initiate scholarly exchanges was made in 1978, even prior to normalization of relations, and the activity, which quickly leap-frogged from academic curiosity to extensive scientific and technical cooperation, continues to be a vital link in the relationship between the United States and China. By

---

[4] According to Huang, during 1964–1966 the Ministry of Education drew up a three-year plan to send 2,000 students abroad to study foreign languages; between 1972 and 1976, 1,629 students were sent abroad (Huang, "A Chinese View," p. 226).

[5] *Zhongguo Gaodeng Xuexiao Jianjie* (*Brief Introduction to China's Institutes of Higher Education*) (Beijing: Education Science Press, 1982, p. 9). By way of confirmation, in 1984 the Ministry of Education reported that China sent more than 33,000 students abroad between 1978 and 1984 (*CD*, Nov. 26, 1984, p. 3) and that this number is more than twice that of students sent abroad between 1949 and 1978, or approximately 16,000 to 17,000. Other scattered data suggest a similar range for the first three decades.

[6] For example, under the U.S.–PRC Agreement on Cooperation in Science and Technology, 26 protocols and memoranda of understanding have been signed between Chinese and U.S. government agencies. For a list of these broad-ranging agreements, see, for example, U.S. Congress, Office of Technololgy Assessment, *Technology Transfer to China*, OTA-ISC-340 (Washington, D.C.: U.S. Government Printing Office, July 1987), pp. 109–112.

now there is no doubt that the United States has played an important role, both in substance and mode, in the economic, academic, and perhaps even political changes that have taken place in China in the 1980s.

What follows is China's perspective on the foreign education issue, as filtered through U.S.-made lenses. Specifically, Part I looks at three basic concerns of Chinese officials: first, developing policies to train people abroad, with special emphasis on the selection process and the changing criteria as dictated by changing needs and circumstances within China; second, the question of a potential "brain drain" and efforts to guarantee the return of students after they complete their studies; and third, the appropriate utilization of foreign-trained scholars once they return home. Since the United States has by far the largest number of Chinese students (and the largest number who choose not to return home), it is safe to assume that when new policies and directives on sending students abroad are considered, it is the United States which is uppermost in the minds of Chinese leaders.

RESUMING THE EXCHANGES

China's post-Mao decision to resume the sending of students abroad for study other than language was made in June 1978 and was undoubtedly hastened by the ambitious plans for scientific development announced at the National Science Conference held in Beijing in March of that year. Whereas the earlier, cautious contacts and exchanges with the West were, at least in part, prompted by the perceived threat from the Soviet Union, the post-Mao leadership quickly shifted its priorities from strategic concerns to the accelerated program for national modernization. The new direction made it clear to Beijing that if the "special scientific and technical spheres" and "pace-setting disciplines," identified at the Science Conference as essential to China's modernization, were to be realized, then the country would have to turn to the industrialized nations of the world for various types of assistance, support, and know-how. The opening of China has indeed created a whole range of channels through which scientific and technical knowledge, experience, and information have been flowing into the country and generating economic and social changes—albeit not always welcome changes—which could not have been foreseen a decade earlier. One of the important channels for the absorption of knowledge in its broadest sense has been and continues to be the exchange of scholars and students between China and the advanced nations of the world.[7]

Although the flow of Chinese students to the United States was on a much larger scale, it was representative of the influx to other countries as well. Chinese scholars started to come here almost immediately after the Nixon visit to China in 1972, but in those early years the visits were primarily short-term get-acquainted tours, which did not evolve into more serious long-term exchanges of scholars and students until the end of the decade. Nevertheless, the importance of academic exchanges in the normalization process can be appreciated by the fact that the Understanding on Educational Exchanges, an agreement that provided for study and research by undergraduate students, graduate students, and visiting scholars, was signed in the fall of 1978—even prior to the establishment of diplomatic relations in January 1979, when it was incorporated into the much broader Agreement on Cooperation in Science and Technology. The current Accord for Educational Exchanges was signed, after much negotiation, in July 1985 and its principles form the basis for all official educational exchanges between the United States and the People's Republic of China.

In principle, access to U.S. educational institutions was an ideal shortcut to the acquisition of world-level scientific and technical knowledge; in practice, however, there were a number of reasons why several years passed before China could take full advantage of the opportunity. Aside from the normal problems of getting a major new program on track, the Chinese had to overcome a more formidable obstacle: the lasting and now all too familiar effects of the Cultural Revolution on the educational system and on the intellectual (educated) segment of the society. Most of the worker-, peasant-, and soldier-students who pursued the much simplified and shortened curricula of Chinese colleges in the 1970s were in no sense qualified to be sent abroad for study.[8]

Consequently, the first wave of Chinese who were sent abroad in the 1970s and early 1980s were, for the most part, scholars in their

---

[7]See, for example, Leo A. Orleans, "Chinese Students and Technology Transfer," *Journal of Northeast Asian Studies*, Vol. IV, No. 4, Winter 1985, pp. 3–25.

[8]For a discussion of the varying qualifications of graduates of Chinese universities, see Leo A. Orleans, "Graduates of Chinese Universities: Adjusting the Total," *The China Quarterly*, September 1987, pp. 444–449.

forties, fifties, and older—virtually all of them from the institutes of the Chinese Academy of Sciences or from universities under the Ministry of Education (now the State Education Commission). They had been trained in the West or in Japan prior to 1949, in the Soviet Union during the 1950s, or in China between 1950 and 1965. They were individuals of professional stature in the research organizations and/or with considerable rank within the bureaucracies of these institutions, but for over a dozen years they had been isolated from the world's scholarly community. For the most part they came to catch up with advances that had taken place in their disciplines. They came to renew old contacts and to establish new ones. Some even managed to pursue research and/or advanced degrees.

There were also a few hundred undergraduates in the early exchanges, but they, too, were somewhat older, primarily individuals who managed to get an education *despite* the Cultural Revolution (usually with the assistance and encouragement of educated parents) and who excelled in the early college-entrance examinations. These circumstances are clearly evident in the figures of the late 1970s. Of the 2,230 individuals who were sent abroad (to all countries) in 1978 and 1979, only 420 (less than a fifth) were undergraduates, 180 were graduate students, and the rest were researchers or scholars.[9]

In general, there was no carefully thought-out policy in those early years for sending students abroad—just a natural extension of the broad-based national goal of modernization and opening up to the West. The aim was to get as many students and scholars into foreign universities and research institutions as Chinese funding and foreign scholarships would allow. The policies evolved gradually through trial and error and through experience. It was natural for U.S. universities to make special arrangements for visiting scholars from China, but in the early years there was also an attempt to bypass normal channels by seeking specialized access. Partly because of the novelty of the relationship with China and the idea of having Chinese students on campus, preferential treatment was often granted. Many U.S. universities acknowledged that special criteria were applied to Chinese students, most notably by waiving some of the standardized tests such as the Test of English as a Foreign Language (TOEFL), which is normally required of all foreign students who are not native speakers of English. Language tests given by the

---

[9] *Beijing Review* (hereafter referred to as *BR*), No. 47, Nov. 23, 1979, p. 5.

Chinese themselves were obviously inadequate because most visiting scholars who came to the United States in 1979 and the early 1980s had serious language deficiencies and had to be enrolled in language training courses. Many institutions also waived the Graduate Record Examination (GRE), the Scholastic Aptitude Test (SAT), and some of the tests required by professional schools. In order to facilitate Chinese access to funding, some specialized groups even set up their own testing process. Universities considered the special treatment of Chinese students to be temporary in nature to facilitate the resumption of exchanges with China—a kind of international "head start" program.[10]

With some prodding and explaining by U.S. academics, it took the Chinese only a year or two to realize that, in the long term, insistence on continued preferential treatment of Chinese students would, in many respects, be counterproductive. Not only would it create obvious problems in relations between them and other students, but preferential treatment would also make it more difficult for Chinese students to compete for financial support. In a significant breakthrough, the Chinese government relented not just by tightening their own national examinations but more significantly by permitting the administering of both TOEFL and GRE in China to anyone hoping to study in the United States. The 1980s also saw an impressive qualitative improvement in Chinese institutions of higher education, thus greatly expanding the pool of individuals who could qualify for admission to foreign universities.

EXPERIENCE AND CHANGE

Naturally, the experiences of Chinese students and scholars sent abroad were studied by the governmental and academic entities involved in foreign education. The review process was continuous, but many of the problems and decisions with regard to sending people abroad were discussed and summarized at periodic national conferences. Although sketchily reported, the information that came out of these conferences reflects some of the indecisions and the gradual evolution of China's policies.

The first national work conference on sending people to study

---

[10]See, for example, Thomas Fingar and Linda A. Reed, *Survey Summary: Students and Scholars from the People's Republic of China in the United States* (Washington, D.C.: U.S.–China Education Clearing House, August 1981).

abroad was called in January 1980 by the Ministry of Education, the State Council, and the Bureau of Scientific and Technical Personnel. It was presided over by Gao Yi, Vice-Minister of Education, and attended by more than 160 people from both national and provincial educational, scientific, and technological departments and commissions. The conferees reiterated the need for foreign training in order to close the gap between China and the advanced countries and confirmed the priorities that were already being followed. Specifically, in selecting "outstanding talent" to send abroad, officials were urged to follow the "three-priority principle":

1.   It is important to select people who will improve the teaching quality of higher education.

2.   While social sciences and language training are important, priority should be given to natural sciences.

3.   Within the natural sciences priority should be given to technological sciences, but without ignoring the needs for either basic science or applied technology.

In 1980, the conferees were also told that all those selected for training abroad had to "support the party line, ardently love the motherland, be dedicated to the revolutionary cause"—a heuristic requirement that seems to have been almost entirely ignored since then.

Two additional points made at that meeting, and frequently repeated since then, looked to the future. First, all were reminded that sending students and scholars abroad was not a short-term policy but one that would continue indefinitely—suggesting that scholarly intercourse with other nations was considered vital to China's long-term modernization goals and not just a temporary, stopgap measure; and second, it was pointed out that, although of necessity in 1980 most of those going abroad were mid-career scholars, in the future most would be graduate students.[11] This transition took several years but, as we shall see, it is now being implemented.

Undoubtedly there were other meetings held in the early 1980s, but the second major conference called to discuss government plans for selecting, administering, educating, and financing students going abroad was held in Beijing in November 1984 and was attended by 270 participants.[12] Although the conference was highly publicized, relatively few details came out of the seven-day meeting.   There

---

[11]Xinhua, Jan. 4, 1980; FBIS, Jan. 9, 1980, p. 4.
[12]CD, Nov. 30, 1984, p. 1.

was, however, a clearly discernible shift in emphasis. By 1984 China reported the return of some 14,000 students (see Table 4-1), and so while problems of selection and financing continued to occupy the conferees, much more time was spent on policies and directives to improve the utilization of those who had returned, balancing their expectations with the needs of national development.[13] Significantly, though not surprisingly, it became clear that foreign education was of prime concern not only to the leaders in the fields of science and technology, education, and economics, but also to the country's political hierarchy, many of whom attended the conference. In fact, Zhang Jingfu, the State Councilor who addressed the opening and closing ceremonies, stated specifically that the principles, targets, problems, and other issues relating to the sending of students abroad were of great concern to the CPC Central Committee and the State Council and that members of these bodies held periodic meetings "to discuss and guide the program."

Perhaps as a consequence of decisions made at the November conference, in early January 1985 the State Council published a set of regulations that, although not too different from earlier directives, marked a somewhat more liberal phase in facilitating foreign training for any individual who was able to "obtain financial support or scholarships in foreign exchange and the necessary enrollment papers." Such individuals could apply to study abroad at any academic level, whether as undergraduates or as advanced scholars, "irrespective of school record, age, or duration of employment."[14] The regulations guaranteed passports not only for students at the undergraduate and graduate levels, but also for individuals already in the work force. The process was further facilitated by the establishment of an office at the Beijing Languages Institute, which would provide consultations to students intending to study abroad. Although, as we shall see, the actual implementation of this policy turned out to be uneven, 1985 and 1986 saw significant increases in the number of U.S. visas issued to Chinese scholars and students (see Table 4-3). The new regulations had two additional benefits. First, with greater reliance on foreign funding the number of students sent abroad could be increased. Second, they relieved Chinese authorities of the difficult and often sensitive selection process by formally passing on the

---

[13]Xinhua, Nov. 29, 1984; FBIS, Nov. 30, 1984, pp. 7–9.
[14]*CD*, Jan. 14, 1985, p. 3.

final responsibility to foreign educational institutions that admit the students—which in practice had already been the case.

The more liberal policies introduced in 1985 only intensified the "study-abroad fever" that was sweeping the urban educational institutions, causing Chinese officials to complain that the students' "blind desire" to study abroad had become "their major objective in life." Writing in a higher education journal, one commentator described it as an abnormal phenomenon deserving serious attention. He noted that in 1985 there was a sharp increase in the number of students taking the TOEFL examination to study abroad on their own.[15] Students expended so much energy in making the right contacts (e.g., approaching foreign scholars visiting their universities) and on foreign language study that their other courses were adversely affected. To counteract this "study-abroad fever" the author stressed the importance of making students understand that a foreign degree—no matter the academic standing of the institution—is not necessarily a guarantee of success and that the level of both undergraduate and graduate studies at some of China's better key universities was comparable to education in foreign countries. China's first-rate universities should not be turned into "study-abroad prep schools," he said, suggesting that this problem could be corrected by improving the overall guidance and direction of students hoping to go abroad, strengthening their ideological and political education, and convincing them that foreign degrees are not the only road to success.[16] The fact is that, while foreign degrees may not be the only road to success, they definitely smooth the bumps and pave the potholes. One commentator writing in the *People's Daily*, for example, congratulated two young men who were awarded French state doctorates in mathematics and were thereupon appointed to professorships at home, but then went on to lament that young persons with similar intelligence and capabilities, but with degrees from Chinese universities, would never be so honored.[17] It will surely take

---

[15]The increase in the number taking the TOEFL examination was primarily due to two factors: (1) in 1985 additional TOEFL centers were opened in China to meet the existing demand, and (2) by then more people had more years of language study.

[16]Xiao Hang, "Do Not Disregard 'Study Abroad Fever'," *Gaojiao Zhanxian* (*Higher Education Front*), No. 3, March 13, 1986; JPRS-CPS-86-058, July 10, 1986, p. 39.

[17]*CD*, April 25, 1987, p. 4.

more than ideological education to overcome the special prestige accorded to foreign diplomas, and it will be a long time before the "study-abroad fever" subsides.

It is not surprising that the preoccupation with foreign study combined with shifting policies created confusion and spawned rumors. No doubt this condition was discussed at the National Conference on Study Abroad in May 1986, which was called to review the program and plan its future course.[18] It was at this conference that Liu Zhongde, Deputy Minister of the State Education Commission, conducted a lengthy interview with reporters from Xinhua news agency and with an education newspaper, *Zhongguo Jiaoyu Bao*— because "so many people were unclear about the country's policies on overseas studies." Curiously, neither source published this important interview until early July.[19]

One of the widespread rumors that Liu had to squelch was that permission to go abroad required leaving a deposit of 20,000 yuan (then about U.S.$8,000) with the government. He gave his assurance that there was no basis for this rumor. Liu did point out, however, that when study tours were financed by a work unit (rather than the state), the students going abroad would have to agree in writing to return to that unit on completion of their foreign studies.[20] Another rumor that had to be dispelled by the State Education Commission was that China planned to reduce the number of students going abroad. "There are no plans to curb the rise in applications for foreign study and research," said the deputy minister, because this program is "in line with the country's policy of opening to the outside world."[21] Nevertheless, reports that Chinese authorities were considering steps to cut back or cut off privately sponsored study abroad persisted and fueled the urgency to get out before any policy changes might be instituted. It is easy to see how the confusion in China would spread to foreign institutions of higher education, where uncertainty was also a problem for university administrators and other officials involved with Chinese students.

Liu Zhongde's interview also included a most authoritative statement on the existing regulations regarding foreign education—regu-

---

[18]Huang, "A Chinese View," p. 249.

[19]*Zhongguo Jiaoyu Bao (China Education News)*, July 8, 1986; JPRS-CPS-86-081, Nov. 6, 1986; see also Xinhua, July 8, 1986; FBIS, July 9, 1986, p. K12.

[20]Xinhua, July 8, 1986; FBIS, July 9, 1986, p. K12.

[21]*CD*, May 15, 1986, p. 3.

lations that were introduced after a six-month survey by the State Education Commission, which began at the end of 1985. The following list summarizes his most important points, which are still valid and have been reiterated by other officials, including then Vice-Premier Li Peng in an interview with Hong Kong correspondents.[22]

1. During the Seventh Five-Year Plan (1986–1990) the number of persons to be sent abroad to study at the expense of the central government will remain approximately at the 1985–1986 level. Nevertheless, the total number of students going abroad is likely to increase because, beginning in 1986, a large proportion of slots for postgraduate studies abroad are being allocated to "various localities, departments, and units using their own funds."

2. The emphasis will be on disciplines in which China has a shortage and that are most important for the country's modernization. The relegation of the selection process to localities will facilitate this goal. First, as in the case of centrally selected scholars, it will be possible for individual work units to insist on a more direct link between foreign education and the specific needs of the sponsoring enterprises and institutions. And second, the units will be able to enter into an agreement with the person sent abroad, in which both parties will have a clear idea of their responsibilities, liabilities, and rights. (A recent dispatch from Beijing, published in the *South China Morning Post* (Hong Kong), stated that the government now requires each student sent abroad by their institution to sign a contract naming a guarantor to financially promise their return. The article cited an incident in which the courts imposed an enormous fine on the wife and family of a student who failed to return from Japan.[23] At this time it is impossible to verify this report or to speculate whether this is a special case or a harbinger of things to come.)

3. Beijing will gradually decrease the number of college graduates going abroad to study for master degrees, while increasing the number going for doctorates after completing the master's at home. As for students who receive doctoral degrees abroad, they must return to China to "work for some time" (other sources say two years) in a university or a research unit before going abroad again for postdoctoral work. This will (again) help the scholars coordinate their

---

[22]*Liaowang Overseas Edition* (Hong Kong), No. 51, Dec. 22, 1986; JPRS-CPS-87-011, March 13, 1987, pp. 25–29.

[23]*South China Morning Post,* March 15, 1988; FBIS-CHI-88-050, March 15, 1988, p. 9.

advanced work with China's needs. At the same time, special funds will be allocated for holders of doctorates, so that they will be able to carry on exchanges with foreign experts and, if necessary, go abroad to participate in academic conferences and postdoctoral research.

4. Liu stressed the need to maintain the highest professional, language, and moral standards for the state-sponsored scholars going abroad. In addition to the obvious reasons for such a requirement, there is another consideration that he did not mention. Chinese government fellowships are now usually limited to one year, and it is the (unstated) expectation of the sponsoring units that Chinese students will be so outstanding that additional education will be financed by grants from the host universities. This is, in fact, a common occurrence (see Tables 5-4, 5-5, and 5-9).

5. His final point referred to those studying abroad at their own expense. On the one hand, he proclaimed that the government will not stand in their way and that they will receive "the same solicitude and care" as the government-sponsored students; on the other hand, he introduced a number of exceptions. More effort will be made, he said, "to guide and control" self-supporting students "so that their selection and dispatch will conform to state requirements, meet certain goals, and be carried out in a planned way." In fact, the suggested controls apply primarily to graduate students enrolled in Chinese universities, who "cannot apply for permission to go abroad to study at their own expense." Without such a restriction, according to Liu, graduate students would drop out of schools, "rush abroad," and upset the existing plans and quotas for domestic postgraduate education. From other sources it is clear, however, that the authorities are attempting to "have their cake and eat it too." The plan is to insist that graduate students with private funding apply for education abroad through the normal government channels and in that capacity apply for official (J-1) visas, to become "self-supported and state-dispatched" *(gongpai zifei)* students. This should relieve the state of the financial burden for their education and, if precedent is a guide, make it more likely that they return after completing their studies.

Liu Zhongde's lengthy interview in May 1986 was, in a sense, a trial balloon. As Deputy Minister, his statements carried all the necessary authority and were undoubtedly passed down through both government and party channels for implementation, but there was no official document to refer to. Perhaps the student demonstrations late that winter and the subsequent speculation about their effects on the sending of students abroad prompted Beijing to publish a formal document to confirm the continued importance of foreign education and to set down the rules and regulations that govern it. This document, which amplifies Liu's points but does not contradict him or others writing in the past year, is entitled "Certain Interim Provisions of the State Education Commission on the Work of Sending Personnel Abroad."[24] The complete text of the "provisions," which were approved by the Party Central Committee and the State Council and released in June 1987 by the State Education Commission, is included in the Appendix.

In the spring of 1988, there was another flurry of rumors about new policies on sending students abroad. Chinese students in the United States cited a document issued on November 28, 1987 (but not released) that includes the following points:

1.   The number of state-sponsored students sent abroad will be reduced to 3,000 per year and only 20 percent of this total (600) will be allowed to come to the United States.

2.   Work units will be limited to sending scholars and not degree candidates.

3.   ". . . [N]o one at work or study is allowed to solicit scholarships, student loans, or any other financial support from foreign or domestic institutions."

4.   Individuals with bachelor's degrees will be limited to two years for a master's degree or five years for a doctor's degree, while those who already have a master's will have to get their PhD in four years.

5.   Postdoctoral research or practical training will be limited to one-and-a-half years.

The students responded with a letter to Premier Li Peng. After assuring him that "Chinese students overseas all love their country," they complained that students abroad were not consulted before policy changes were made, pointed to the unrealistic nature of the new regulations, and requested that the new restrictions be reexamined.

In early April 1988, Huang Xinbai, a member of the State Education Commission, addressed the students' concern by stating that China's policy of sending students abroad "remains unchanged and

---

[24]Xinhua, June 10, 1987; JPRS-CAR-87-024, July 23, 1987, p. 89. Given the volatility of the subject, the word "interim" is likely to remain in the title of any future revisions of this document.

will never change."[25] He went on to note that reports of cuts were groundless and "fabricated with ulterior motives" and that in 1988 the number of students going abroad will be approximately as they were in 1987 (i.e., about 3,000 state-sponsored, about 5,000 unit-sponsored, and a minimum of 3,000 self-financed). Huang did not reject the figure of 600 state-financed students coming to the United States, but explained that 4,000 others will come under the auspices of the various institutions and work units. Huang admitted, however, that some "adjustments" will be made, essentially corresponding to earlier-discussed policies: increasing the number going abroad to pursue advanced studies, encouraging applied rather than theoretical fields of study, and sending more students to countries that, so far, have accepted few Chinese.

How should this latest exchange between the students and the State Education Commission be interpreted? It is premature and therefore risky to make any definite conclusions. Two points, however, should be kept in mind. First, Chinese students in the United States have had a tendency to be overly sensitive to every decree or rumor emanating from home and, not surprisingly, translate them immediately in terms of their own personal and professional concerns. And second, although theoretically the State Education Commission is the officially designated agency to oversee the sending of students abroad, it admits that all it can provide is guidance and suggestions and that it has no way of controlling students sent by other ministries and organizations. It is therefore reasonable to expect that whether significant changes in China's policies are taking place, as the students maintain, or changes are not anticipated, as the authorities in Beijing profess, the broad chasm that has existed between official proclamations and local interpretation and implementation will still be there, a divergence discussed in detail in the next section.

PROBLEMS OF IMPLEMENTATION

Since, on the face of it, each set of regulations seemed to answer most of the questions generated by the studies-abroad program, why then has there been so much confusion both in China and in the host countries? Why is there a continuing divergence between a stated

---

[25]Press release, Embassy of the People's Republic of China, Washington, D.C., April 8, 1988.

policy and how it is actually implemented? A few reasons can be suggested.

As in the case of so many recent policies, regulations on foreign education are not only new but, as we have seen, constantly evolving to match changing needs, attitudes, and experiences. Communications being what they are in China, new regulations promulgated in Beijing do not always travel through the same channels or reach the relevant units at the same time, or even in the same form. To further confuse the issue, individual localities and institutions are encouraged to interpret and implement all policies "according to local conditions." Moreover, as we already know, regulations and procedures for state-sponsored students have differed from those for privately sponsored students. It is therefore entirely possible that several institutions in the same city may not be implementing policies in the same way and that two students from adjacent universities could receive different instructions regarding foreign study. Such cumulative distortion of policies provides fertile ground for rumors and confusion.

Additional complications result from the inevitable exceptions. Some students have complained that they were not permitted to leave the country even after assurance of funding and admission to a foreign university. The directive that requires students to work before going abroad has been implemented helter-skelter in some localities and ignored in others. Nor did it help that offspring of high-level officials seemed unencumbered by the rules and had little difficulty in going abroad for both undergraduate and graduate degrees.[26] Despite adverse publicity, it appears that this practice did not disappear completely and rumor has it that new regulations will be introduced regarding senior cadres' children studying abroad at their own expense.[27] Moreover, decentralized funding patterns—both

---

[26]See, for example, David Wong and Ian Chung, "Who Gets To Study Abroad," *Hong Kong Standard,* Nov. 3, 1986; FBIS, Nov. 5, 1986, p. K5. This article lists the names of several dozen students from families of high-ranking officials who went abroad to study, as well as the institutions that they attended. While it is true that these parents were more likely to be able to subsidize foreign education and to speed up the necessary paperwork, it is only fair to say that, by virtue of their environment and opportunities, children of high-ranking cadres are more likely to meet the academic requirements for admission to foreign universities than are most Chinese youth.

[27]*Cheng Ming* (Hong Kong), Jan. 1, 1988; FBIS-CHI-88-003, Jan. 6, 1988, p. 18.

local and from abroad—make it difficult for the central government to control the flow of students. The various obstacles on the home front, of course, are further accentuated by the uncertainties associated with the difficult process of obtaining visas. It is not surprising, therefore, that so many prospective students for foreign education are confused, nervous, and perplexed about their future.

What seems clear is that as long as the "study-abroad fever" continues and the current mood and attitudes persist, the ingenious Chinese youth will inevitably be searching for (and often finding) ways and means of circumventing any regulations that may stand in the way. The liberalization of the economy and the impressive advances made in higher education in recent years may moderate the "study-abroad fever," but it is not likely to stem the desire of young intellectuals for a foreign education.

2
The Brain-Drain Issue

The value of sending thousands of students abroad is self-evident, but the policy is not without considerable risks. Not unlike the Chinese Viceroy, who in 1858 observed, "When the Emperor rules over so many millions, what does he care for the few waifs that have drifted away to a foreign land?"[1] Deng Xiaoping also speculated, during his 1980 visit to the United States, that the inevitability of some students not returning should not negate the value of the exchange programs. This has been the standard response by Chinese officials for some years, but as the number of students and scholars going abroad has grown, so, too, has the number choosing, at best, to delay their return and, at worst, to change their visa status and not to return at all. Beijing's concern is understandable, for the country is no longer losing waifs, after all, but the cream of China's youth. And, as the Chinese officials like to point out, it is often the most talented individuals who manage to find a way to remain abroad, or at least to postpone their return.

Although, as we shall see, the loss of students to foreign countries has been essentially limited to those who were privately funded, the acute concern is evident in official statements and reflected in

---

[1] Mary Roberts Coolidge, *Chinese Immigration* (New York, Arno Press, 1909), p. 57.

the many articles on the subject in various Chinese journals. Recent college graduates have been chastised for ignoring the needs of the country and applying for further study abroad as soon as they are assigned a job. One commentator propounded that too many students go abroad "to 'pan for gold,' 'become gold-plated,' and 'worship money'" and China can no longer "sit back and relax" and let "one by one the bees and butterflies fly across the wall."[2]

Be that as it may, the State Education Commission now believes that enough significant progress has been made in upgrading higher education at home to change the makeup of students and scholars going abroad and thereby to at least decrease the likelihood that they will not return. Clearly, with approximately 2 million students enrolled in institutions of higher education, for most disciplines undergraduate study abroad is a luxury. More important, the previously almost nonexistent graduate education has also expanded and improved. Enrollment of graduate students increased from 21,600 in 1980 to 110,000 in 1986[3] and, according to He Dongchang, serving in his capacity as Vice-President of the State Council's Academic Degrees Committee, between 1981 and 1987 China granted 53,300 MAs and 664 PhDs.[4] Reflecting this development, a recent circular issued by the State Education Commission stated that "China will mainly rely on its own efforts to train graduate students and set up a graduate education system with distinct Chinese characteristics."[5] As graduate schools expand and improve, China is essentially limiting foreign education to PhD and postdoctorate students and scholars. This means, of course, that a decision to remain abroad by these more highly trained individuals would not only be a loss to the country, in terms of both money spent on their education and their potential contribution to China's development, but also be a painful loss of face. It is somewhat ironic that the already mentioned policy, which limits government funding to one or two years and expects the students to find their own financial support through foreign sources, runs counter to the new expectations—loosening the bonds to the motherland and promoting the kind of independence and self-sufficiency that could encourage students to remain abroad.

---

[2] *Liaowang (Outlook)*, No. 10, March 10, 1986; JPRS-ECPS-86-055, June 16, 1986, pp. 65–66.

[3] *BR*, No. 9, Feb. 2, 1987, p. 25.

[4] *CD*, Nov. 16, 1987, p. 3.

[5] Xinhua, Dec. 20, 1986; JPRS-CPS-87-010, Feb. 27, 1987, p. 26.

Finally, it is worth noting the obvious; China's brain-drain problem would be insignificant were it not for the United States. This being the case, it is important to distinguish clearly between scholars and students sponsored (but not always paid for) by the Chinese government (J-1 visas) and students who go abroad using private funds (F-1 visas).

GOVERNMENT-SPONSORED
STUDENTS AND SCHOLARS

The U.S. Embassy and Consulates in China issue J-1 visas to individuals who are formally nominated by the Chinese government or research or work units (and approved by the government) and who have obtained an IAP-66 form to show that they have qualified under one of the programs designated by the U.S. Information Agency (USIA). A large proportion of the J-1 visa holders are scholars or professors already established in their fields (mostly in science and engineering) who go abroad for advanced study, or they are managers and other officials sent by their work units for more specialized technical study.[6] The number of undergraduates with J-1 visas has decreased even further since then. In a 1986 article, Li Peng, then Minister of the State Education Commission, once again emphasized that state selection of students for study abroad should focus primarily on advanced students and scholars and that "we will not send undergraduate students abroad, except for those studying languages or other specialized subjects."[7]

The most important point to be made with regard to the holders of J-1 visas is that, at least through 1986, the overwhelming majority have been returning to China on completion of their programs. This is the explicit belief of the legal staff of the USIA, and it is supported by the statistics on J-1 visas presented in the second half of this

---

[6]Chinese sources report that by the end of 1984, 78 percent of state-financed individuals were "taking refresher courses" (i.e., scholars catching up with developments in their fields that occurred during the decade of the Cultural Revolution, when China was isolated from world scholarship), 18 percent were graduate students, and only 4 percent were undergraduates (Xinhua, Nov. 28, 1984; JPRS-CPS-84-089, Dec. 19, 1984, p. 39). These figures differ from visa statistics presented and discussed in Part II of this study.

[7]Li Peng, "Some Issues Concerning the Reform and Development of Higher Education," *Zhongguo Gaodeng Jiaoyu* (*China's Higher Education*), No. 7, July 13, 1986; JPRS-CPS-86-085, Dec. 12, 1986, p. 1.

study. In part, this is due to the "two-year rule," which states that, with very few exceptions, holders of J-1 visas cannot change to immigrant status without first leaving the United States for at least two years. According to the Immigration and Naturalization Service (INS), since 1982 only 265 state-sponsored J-1 visa holders managed to adjust their status: 35 in 1982, 43 in 1983, 20 in 1984, 50 in 1985, 53 in 1986, and 64 in 1987. In contrast, the numbers of F-1 visa holders who adjusted their status during the same years were 1,895 in 1982, 1,163 in 1983, 607 in 1984, 739 in 1985, 825 in 1986, and 744 in 1987, for a total of 5,973.[8] Nevertheless, both sides seem to agree that the seeds of a more difficult problem are present. Beijing complains that despite presumed legal restrictions, scholars on J-1 visas are managing to change their status or to extend their stay in the United States. The unofficial U.S. response is that as long as they remain students and do nothing illegal, no one will seek them out for deportation.

The early arrivals were usually older scholars who were professionally secure and with family ties. They could be fairly sure, based on the experience of others, that a year or two spent abroad would further enhance their positions within their institutions or otherwise advance their careers.[9] China's current concern is with the younger graduate students who are now completing their studies. These young scholars, many of whom are not attached to wife, children, or work unit, ostensibly are more apt to search for ways to circumvent the immigration laws in an effort to remain abroad.

PRIVATELY SPONSORED STUDENTS

Whereas J-1 visas are issued to both students and scholars, only students who are not nominated or supported by the Chinese government are issued F-1 visas. The first small group of students went abroad at their own expense as early as 1978—an unheard of

---

[8] Figures for 1982 through 1985 were assembled from *Statistical Yearbook of the Immigration and Naturalization Service* (Washington, D.C.: U.S. Department of Justice); for 1986 and 1987 figures obtained by telephone from the Immigration and Naturalization Service. It is interesting to note that during the same six years fewer than 200 J-1 visa holders but approximately 9,000 F-1 visa holders from Taiwan adjusted their status to permanent resident.

[9] See, for example, Otto Schnepp, University of Southern California, "The Impact of Returning Scholars on Chinese Science and Technology." Report prepared for the National Science Foundation (1984).

occurrence during the preceding 30 years. Since this occasion was publicized in the Chinese media, word spread rapidly and soon large numbers of urban youths who had the necessary scholastic qualifications started searching for well-to-do relatives or friends living abroad. And because by far the largest number of overseas Chinese in the West reside in the United States, it is not surprising that the overwhelming majority of the prospective students managed to find sponsorship in this country. Nevertheless, the number of F-1 visas issued by the U.S. Embassy and Consulates continues to be much smaller than the number requested, in part because of the large proportion of the privately sponsored students who remain in the United States and also, perhaps, because of steps to pacify related Chinese fears. In 1986, for example, the U.S. Embassy and the four U.S. Consulates in China were turning down more than half the F-1 visa applicants. Most were said to have inadequate evidence of financial support and/or were suspected of pursuing emigration, not education. Despite the careful screening the suspicions continue to be confirmed by the large proportion of the F-1 visa holders who, after a year or two in the United States, seek to adjust their status from "student" to "permanent resident."

As already discussed, some of the regulations with regard to self-supported studies abroad fluctuated over the years. For a time, undergraduates were not permitted to leave China until they completed their studies and spent two years working. There were also restrictions with regard to certain professions, such as university lecturers, engineers, and high-level physicians. All these impediments were introduced to decrease the chance of losing specialists already in short supply. In 1985 the reins on self-supporting students were again loosened and, as mentioned earlier, anyone who was accepted by a foreign institution and had the necessary funds could get permission to leave. It is not always possible, however, to match changes in Chinese policies with the fluctuations in the actual number of visas issued.

Privately supported students constitute a serious dilemma for Beijing. Theoretically, they increase the number of foreign-trained specialists at no cost to the state. On the other hand, too many of them opt not to return. Perhaps, however, there is an ameliorating factor to be considered. About one-third of the F-1 students come to the United States as undergraduates. Given the difficulty of passing college-entrance examinations in China and the limited number of university slots, it is possible that many of the students accepted by U.S. colleges had, or would have, failed to get admission into a Chinese institution of higher education. If so, then the loss to China is not quite as great as generally assumed, and it is conceivable that Chinese students with a U.S. degree who choose to remain in the United States are, at least potentially, more useful than if they remained workers in China with a secondary education, especially if the remittances that are customarily sent home are considered. As for those who came here for graduate education, it is very likely that a large proportion of that group, too, would not have been selected to fill the limited number of slots in Chinese graduate schools. And someday they might return.

There is a special problem with regard to F-1 visa holders who do opt to return. The jealousy-inspired discrimination against all returnees is said to be especially bitter toward those whose education was paid for by relatives or friends. Beijing knows that this situation must be corrected before more students with F-1 visas can be enticed to return. Following the 1984 conference on foreign study, the State Council issued detailed Draft Regulations on Self-Supported Study Abroad, which have since been frequently and selectively cited by numerous Chinese officials.[10] In brief, the regulations assure self-supported students who have not returned and those planning to leave that they will be provided equal job opportunities and in general be shown the same consideration as those sent and supported by the state. Complaints of returnees with degrees in scientific and technical fields could be referred to the State Science and Technology Commission's Bureau of Personnel for resolution and placement. Individuals who are leaving jobs for foreign study "may have their posts reserved for them with their pay suspended." Efforts will be made to help them solve any difficulties and problems they might encounter. If necessary, the state will even pay their return fare. One announcement went so far as to encourage these students to express their professional interests and preferred work locations to officials at Chinese embassies and consulates and promised every effort would be made to comply.[11] Inquiries of embassy personnel in Washington, however, indicated that no one was aware of any such regulation nor has any student attempted to take advantage of the offer.

One Hong Kong observer presented an anecdotal, yet usefully

---

[10] Xinhua, Jan. 11, 1985; FBIS, Jan. 15, 1985, pp. 12–15.

[11] See, for example, Zhongguo Xinwen She (China News Agency, Hong Kong), Feb. 10, 1987; FBIS, Feb. 11, 1987, p. K2.

descriptive listing of representative groups of privately sponsored Chinese students in the United States:

1. Earnestly studying.
2. Earned a degree and either planning to continue studies or found a job and seeking to change student status.
3. Not in school, either because never intended to go or because of financial, language, or classroom difficulties; most try to earn money in any way they can and end up becoming illegal immigrants.
4. Another and closely related group uses education as a cover to work and earn money and consists of students who are enrolled in "irregular schools"; they pay their tuition but seldom or never go to class while they look for various opportunities.
5. Individuals who use education as an excuse to get abroad but, once they have done some studying, try to find a way to change their status, with marriage as a frequent shortcut (especially among women students).[12]

Although it could not have been a scientific study, anecdotal information supports the identified categories of privately sponsored students.

THE STUDENTS' PERSPECTIVE

Despite policy fluctuations, it is relatively easy to understand and describe the official position on sending students abroad; to theorize on the rationale behind the individual plans made by tens of thousands of Chinese students contemplating their future is much more problematic. There are two reasons why this discussion is especially speculative at this time. First, since early 1986, the thinking of Chinese students and scholars has been undergoing a transition. Second, whereas statistical evidence on the returnees for the 1979–1986 period is in hand, later data are not yet available. Consequently, how shifting policies and conditions are affecting attitudes and reasons can only be surmised. Nevertheless, it is important to review some factors that students surely must consider as they mull over whether to stay in the United States or return to China.

Given the example of other foreign students who have studied and remained in the United States, it is striking that, at least through

---

[12] *Pai Shing Semi-Monthly* (Hong Kong), Aug. 16, 1985; JPRS-CST-85-038, Nov. 5, 1985, p. 78.

1986, almost all of China's government-sponsored and perhaps one-third of the self-supporting students and scholars who completed their studies returned home (see Part II). Even in 1986, according to a survey of Chinese students in North America, only 9 percent of the 395 respondents indicated that they planned to remain in the West permanently.[13] The Chinese Alliance for Democracy, which took this survey (an organization that is most belligerent in its criticisms of Beijing's policies toward intellectuals) concluded that "if China were only to adopt a policy of progressive liberalization, and provide an increasingly favorable environment for scientists and researchers, there would be no cause to worry that students would not return."

Let us consider first some reasons why Chinese students and scholars have been returning and then examine some of the factors influencing them to remain in this country.

Aside from the legal impediments to be overcome, there are strong push-and-pull factors that account for most foreign students' return home. There is attachment to family, friends, and familiar surroundings. There is the attractive prospect of being "a big fish" (though probably in a much smaller pond), which is usually the status they return to. For the Chinese student, improved economic and social conditions at home should make the decision to return easier than it might have been some years ago. On the "push" side, there is the accumulation of problems associated with living in and adjusting to a new country. There is also the difficulty of acquiring proficiency in a complicated foreign language that is a prerequisite to success in most professions—a problem which is particularly aggravated for those who tend to spend their free time in Chinese enclaves. No doubt reflecting his own feelings while studying in Moscow in the 1950s, Li Peng affirmed that "studying abroad is a painful experience," just as it was for Chinese students in the Soviet Union.[14]

Only a few years ago China observers would not have hesitated to list yet another set of reasons for Chinese students to return home, even though for those who did not have a sense of China, these reasons would have been difficult to understand. In the late 1980s these additional reasons may seem especially outdated—and yet, because

---

[13] "A Survey on China's Policy Toward Studying Abroad," *China Spring Digest,* July–August 1987, pp. 39–41; translated by J. A. Williams from the January 1987 issue of *Chung-kuo Chih-ch'un (China Spring).*

[14] *Liaowang Overseas Edition* (Hong Kong), No. 51, Dec. 22, 1986; JPRS-CPS-87-011, March 13, 1987.

of their proven timelessness, they cannot be ignored. To Americans, many of the strongest motivations for Chinese students and scholars to return home may seem foreign or out-of-date—loyalty, patriotism, a desire to contribute to the development and modernization of their country, and a feeling of obligation for expenses incurred by the state and/or work unit in sending them abroad. These reasons are often disregarded, not only because they seem almost quaint in today's milieu, but also because they parallel Beijing's polemic. In China's case, it is a mistake. The ingrained pride associated with being a part of the oldest continuous historical and cultural entity is very real for the Chinese people. Propaganda that extolls the virtues of being Chinese and living in China is a needless reminder—especially for Chinese intellectuals. A survey of Chinese students in the United States showed the overwhelming proportion intend to return home and, according to the survey, the main reason for this decision is "because they are Chinese." [15]

The China "magnet" is not new. Of the millions who migrated in the past hundred years, the overwhelming proportion left not because of a special attraction for or the "pull" of foreign lands, but because of the "push" created by the inordinately difficult economic and political conditions in their homeland.[16] And if these same circumstances prevented them from returning sooner, most hoped to be buried in their native province or village. The historical and cultural factors which translate into a traditional attachment to the motherland may be less visible among the much more sophisticated Chinese students now in the United States, but for most of them, nationalism and the desire to be part of a Chinese renaissance are still present.

Conversely, China's "brain-drain" concerns would be baseless if there were not compelling reasons to remain in the United States. Career considerations would be paramount for scientists and engineers, who would undoubtedly find greater professional satisfaction

---

[15]*CD*, Aug. 15, 1986, p. 3. It is no wonder that this survey by a Taiwan-educated scholar was picked up in the Beijing press.

[16]A colorful contradiction to this statement was expressed by two Chinese Treaty Commissioners in 1880: "Being from a race of dwellers upon the seacoast, they [Chinese laborers] have desired to go thither and have regarded California as a land of abundance and as furnishing great opportunities. They have also rejoiced in the freedom of the United States. Hence they have not gone there as a result of deceit, or by being kidnapped, nor under contract as coolies, but have flown thither as the wild geese fly." As cited in Mary Roberts Coolidge, *Chinese Immigration* (New York, Arno Press, 1909), p. 49.

here—especially in subfields in which China lags behind world levels. Moreover, the attraction of the United States for anyone interested in pursuing basic research is recognized by scientists not only from third world nations but even from Japan—a viewpoint recently expressed by that country's first Nobel Prize winner in medicine. Dr. Tonegawa was quoted as saying that any free-spirited researcher must leave Japan to thrive and that universities in his country are too authoritarian, too focused on seniority, and too inflexible to let young researchers pursue unproved but potentially innovative ideas.[17] This attitude toward undirected research is certainly still prevalent in China, only intensified by funding constraints and the leadership's lack of understanding of the relationship between science and technology.

The enticement of the United States for Chinese students in social sciences, humanities, and the arts (a much larger proportion of whom are supported by private funds) is related to professional freedom of expression—which in China has fluctuated between restricted and nonexistent. The fact that employment in these fields is especially difficult for foreign-born scholars in the United States does not seem to be a major deterrent.

Last, but definitely not least, is the inevitable lure of income and life-style to which all Chinese students can aspire in the United States. In this regard, the self-evident advantages would not be nearly as important were it not for the continuing problems experienced by intellectuals in China. After 10 years of lip service to the intellectual cause, at the Thirteenth CPC National Congress of the Communist Party, then Premier Zhao Ziyang still felt it necessary to repeat that China "must create a social environment in which knowledge and educated people are respected and must continue to improve the working and living conditions of intellectuals so as to turn human resources to best account."[18] The response of intellectuals to such statements is more "loud thunder but small raindrops." In the inflationary environment of the 1980s, their incomes and living conditions have admittedly been improving slower than those of peasants and workers and, according to Zhao Fusan, the Vice-President

---

[17]Clyde Haberman, "Japan Asks Why Scientists Go West to Thrive," *New York Times,* Nov. 11, 1987, p. 9.

[18]General Secretary Zhao Ziyang's report to the Thirteenth National Congress of the Communist Party, Oct. 15, 1987; *BR*, No. 45, Nov. 9–15, 1987, p. 30.

of China's Academy of Social Sciences, "Private traders are making fortunes whereas officials and intellectuals are underpaid."[19] A more vivid description of the plight of intellectuals was provided by a Nanfang University professor: "Now the peasants are standing on a gold brick, the workers on a silver brick, and the intellectuals are wearing a tall hat; they seem taller than the others, but they have no substantial benefits."[20] In more scholarly language, this growing income disparity between intellectuals and the rest of the society is aptly summarized in *Science* by Nicholas Lardy, Professor of Chinese Economics at the University of Washington: "The decline in the incomes of scientists and engineers relative to that of workers in other sectors of the economy, where the opportunities for commercial and entrepreneurial activities have widened steadily and real incomes have grown explosively, has been particularly corrosive."[21] Since this condition applies to all professionals, the students' decision to stay or to return would be made much easier if they saw clear evidence of improvement in the living conditions of intellectuals in China.

As hard as it is to make the decision to remain in the United States, it is, of course, even more challenging to implement it. In the case of Chinese students, however, there are several facilitating factors. The large Chinese population in this country, with it highly educated middle class, offers not only a familiar environment and considerable support, but often employment as well. Furthermore, non-Chinese employers tend to have a high regard for these hard-working and bright individuals, usually survivors of a stiff selection process before they were permitted to leave China. The relative ease with which Chinese students and scholars have been able to find employment and academic fellowships to extend their stay in this country has been a painful thorn in the side of Chinese authorities. Here too, however, a caveat is in order, for the easily obtained scholarships and fellowships do not prepare the Chinese graduate of a U.S. university for the definite limits on career opportunities that exist. If the past experience of foreign students in the United States holds, for each one who will rise to the top, many more are likely to

---

[19]From an interview published in *Le Figaro* (Paris), Oct. 27, 1987; FBIS-CHI-87-213, Nov. 4, 1987, p. 32.
    [20]*Ming Pao* (Hong Kong), Sept. 1, 1987; FBIS-CHI-87-172, Sept. 4, 1987, p. 4.
    [21]*Science*, Jan. 1, 1988, p. 79.

end up as frustrated, unhappy individuals, who will feel they have suffered discrimination in this country.

All of these push-and-pull factors have been reasonably stable over the past decade. Why, then, does an increasing number of students and scholars appear to be choosing to emigrate or at least to postpone their return? It would be too easy to place all the blame on the student demonstrations in China in the winter of 1986. This short-lived turmoil seemed almost an aberration; it was handled gently by the authorities and, by now, most of the overt dissent seems to be limited to a relatively small group of vocal and highly publicized intellectuals. For the overwhelming majority of students, conditions in China appear to be approximately back to where they were before the demonstrations and, one would expect, more professionally appealing now than in the early 1980s. So what has changed? The change is in the characteristics of students and scholars in the United States and how they reflect the new mood in China through their own personalities and goals.

In a sense, students and scholars who came here in the early 1980s were of a different breed. China had only recently emerged from both the physical and communicative isolation of the Cultural Revolution. Going abroad for the first time to study was not simply a unique opportunity but also a wondrous and even mysterious experience. Students and, to a lesser degree, scholars (who were then considerably older than scholars abroad today) seemed understandably apprehensive and much more passive in terms of their own demands and the demands placed on them. In those early years, whether because of conscientiousness, fear, patriotism, or inexperience, few officially sponsored students or scholars are believed to have seriously contemplated remaining permanently in the United States. It is noteworthy that, despite the campaign against "spiritual pollution," almost 3,000 Chinese with J-1 visas returned in 1984 and almost 5,000 returned in 1985 (see Chapter 5).

By the middle 1980s, younger students and scholars were arriving with somewhat different attitudes and perceptions. Again to generalize, many of these later students were only children at the height of the Cultural Revolution. They had attended Chinese secondary schools and universities when political content in the curriculum was nonexistent or, at least, greatly deemphasized. Considered pampered by many in China, most came unencumbered by family or attachment to any work unit. Finally, they not only knew more about what to expect when they got here, but they were much more confident about their ability to compete and succeed in the new environment.

Probably even more important than the changing characteristics of students are the changes that have been taking place in China in the 1980s. Beijing now refers to "Chinese-style socialism," but, admittedly an oversimplification, it might be easier to understand as "practical socialism": if it works, call it socialist and use it. As part of the modernization process, Beijing is attempting to increase productivity in all sectors of the economy through increased incentives, in part by encouraging private venture for those who are outside the work-unit system and by motivating work units, as well as individuals within the units, to sign a variety of contractual agreements that would either boost or supplement salaries. Monetary gain rather than ideology has become the motivating force in China and, in the process, there has been a gradual transition during which national interest became subsumed by a strong sense of individual interest. Ironically, while this liberalized attitude provides a climate more conducive to professional opportunity in China, it has also created an environment of rising expectations that spawned the current crop of students and scholars in the United States and is influencing their final decision to return or to stay.

There are yet other important factors to consider in any attempt to explain why students and scholars now in the United States are more likely than before to seek ways to remain here. It would appear that, despite the complaints of many returnees, those who went back in earlier years had little competition and were therefore much more apt to find themselves in acceptable employment situations. The new graduates of U.S. universities, however, are confronted with totally different conditions. First, the shortage in professional manpower is not nearly as severe as it was, therefore, competition for the more desirable locations (e.g., Shanghai and Beijing) and positions (e.g., institutes of an academy of science) is becoming much keener.[22] Second, large numbers of individuals are getting advanced degrees in fields of science for which in China there is now a shortage of both positions and facilities. And third, the importance of advanced degrees notwithstanding, in the earlier years more undergraduate

---

[22] According to an official of the State Education Commission, "After years of expanding education programmes, the gap between the supply and demand for college graduates is no longer so sharp as before" (*CD*, Oct. 17, 1987, p. 3).

students went abroad; they had lower expectations and were easier to place than the current graduate students.

Chinese students and scholars gradually have overcome the fear of U.S. law and the anticipated embarrassment to themselves and to their country if, by delaying their return, they became involved in legal entanglements and eventual deportation. It took a number of years for them to discover that unless they commit a crime, neither the U.S. Immigration and Naturalization Service nor the local police or the FBI is likely to be on their trail for overstaying their legal time period. Legal concerns continue, but that they are not immediate must be comforting to the students and scholars and an important factor, if not in the final decision, then at least in delaying a decision.

Finally, just as the Chinese people in general, students and scholars seem no longer willing "to eat bitterness." Those who choose to remain in the United States are seeking not only professional fulfillment but also insurance against the eventuality that bitterness will once again be the fare in China. Given the openness with which Chinese officials discuss these problems, their concurrence with this evaluation is a reasonable expectation.

PROSPECTS

As we have already seen, Beijing's understandable concern about the potential brain drain so far has not diminished the number of scholars sent abroad; the emphasis, rather, has been on making changes in the qualifications and specializations of these individuals. As pointed out by then Minister Li Peng, supervision of the students going abroad was inadequate in the past. In the future "students must be sent on a need basis, quality control must be exercised, and there must be an integration of learning and application."[23]

In this connection, in the latter part of 1986, the Science and Technology section of the Chinese Embassy in the United States invited six scholars from China to participate in an informal discussion concerning Chinese students in this country and ways to assure their return. Among the recommendations made by this panel were that only outstanding people be selected from the pool of young and middle-aged research and teaching personnel, that their advanced

---

[23]Li Peng, "Some Issues Concerning the Reform and Development of Higher Education," *Zhongguo Gaodeng Jiaoyu* (*China's Higher Education*), No. 7, July 1986; JPRS-CPS-86-085, Dec. 12, 1986, p. 46.

study program be clearly defined and regularly reviewed, and that the length of time spent in advanced study should be decided on an individual basis. Reemphasized was the familiar demand that research projects be relevant to the needs of the domestic units which sent the individual abroad. Moreover, the panel recommended that when foreign-trained scholars return, they should be assigned work on the basis of ability rather than seniority—when appropriate, skipping salary grades and taking on graduate students of their own. Additionally, officials at the Embassy in Washington and the five Consulates were urged to maintain close contact with Chinese scholars in U.S. universities, assisting them with any academic or personal problems that may arise.[24] This practice is now being implemented more thoroughly than before and a foreign-service person from each Chinese consulate is specifically assigned to perform such functions. The hope is, of course, that personal and frequent contact with each scholar will positively influence that person's "final decision."

As is so often the case, however, while national intent is clearly detailed in a variety of sources, the implementation of the stated policies or regulations may be difficult to discern in practice. For example, the goal of holding the number of self-supporting students to a minimum, and thereby reducing the potential pool of people who might decide to remain abroad, is yet to be reflected in the number of F-1 visas issued, which in fact grew by 68 percent between 1985 and 1986 albeit dropping to a 5 percent increase between 1986 and 1987. The intent to have a larger proportion of scholars doing advanced work in fields other than science and technology, such as management, computer science, and economics and other social sciences, has yet to be reflected in the enrollment statistics.

Another difficult problem now being discussed is how to assure that before going abroad students in scientific and technical disciplines not only attain academic qualifications, but also some work experience in industrial production, research and development, planning and design, and management. To accomplish this, there is now (at least in theory) a two-year work requirement before going abroad, which would produce somewhat older scholars (at least in their mid-

---

[24] "Chinese Scholars on Visit to the United States Regard the Development of Scholarly Leaders as the Major Goal of Sending Personnel Abroad for Study," *Keji Ribao (Science and Technology Daily)*, Jan. 26, 1987; JPRS-CST-87-014, April 6, 1987.

and late-twenties), more established in their professions and work-places, perhaps with families, and therefore more likely to return to China on completion of their academic work.

Since the emphasis on practical experience is supposed to carry over to their studies abroad, Beijing must be aware of the resistance that may be encountered on the U.S. side. Some practical experience is already available to Chinese students, as to all foreign students on J-1 visas, because built into this program is an 18-month visa extension for practical training.[25] The proposed changes, however, suggest a reversal of priorities: practical training is to take precedence over degrees. If that is indeed the case, then it is difficult to see how such programs would fit into the existing curricula of U.S. universities. Could students continue to be enrolled in degree programs while acquiring experience in industrial production and research and development, for example? Will they occupy a sponsored research position at a university, and if so, what would be the motivation for a U.S. institution of higher education to accept such an arrangement? If the intent is to go outside the established academic exchanges to arrange for this type of practical experience, the Chinese have to face the fact that, although many U.S. corporations have been running training programs for the Chinese, U.S. industry generally has not been receptive to placing foreign nationals into research and production positions that might reveal proprietary information that could be channelled to a potentially competitive nation.

Since scholars can play a very important role in technology transfer, China's desire for her students to obtain more hands-on experience in U.S. industries and laboratories may well run into the ever-present security concerns in Washington. These concerns will surely be stimulated by an increased presence of Chinese nationals in private and public research establishments.[26]

Yet another innovation sought by the State Education Commission to fill China's need for highly trained scholars, while hopefully alleviating the returning student problem, is the granting of joint

---

[25]In June 1987 it became unlawful for U.S. employers to hire foreign students who do not have a work permit. This new law should have a significant impact on Chinese students who may try to stay beyond the 18-month visa extension.

[26]See, for example, Larry M. Wortzel, "U.S. Technology Transfer Policies and the Modernization of China's Armed Forces," *Asian Survey*, No. 6, June 1987, pp. 615–637; Leo A. Orleans, "Chinese Students and Technology Transfer," *Journal of Northeast Asian Studies*, Vol. IV, No. 4, Winter 1985, pp. 3–25.

PhD degrees by Chinese and U.S. universities. One suggestion is for students in scientific and technical disciplines to complete three years of postgraduate course work in China (earning MA degrees), spend two years in residence at a U.S. university doing research and laboratory work, and then return to China to write dissertations to be approved by a joint U.S.-PRC faculty committee. In the social sciences the sequence would be reversed, with students doing course work in the United States and then returning to China to do research and write their dissertation. In either case, PhD degrees would not be granted until the student returned to China, thus providing a most tangible reason to return. The problem, of course, is to find a U.S. institution of higher education willing to lend its name to a joint degree over which it would have only partial control. Some have suggested that such an arrangement may be easier to implement with universities in Canada or Europe.

Whatever the problems, and despite the recent flurry of rumors and concerns about severe cuts in the number of scholars and students to be sent to the United States (see Chapter 1), Beijing is not likely to be deterred from sending individuals abroad to obtain advanced degrees and experience. The comments of two individuals, one an official and one a private citizen, seem to bracket the range of reasons for this conclusion. An official perspective was expressed by Fang Yi, State Councilor and former Minister of the State Science and Technology Commission. In an interview with *The China Business Review,* he pointed out that scholars who have returned from the United States have not only become "the backbone in the ranks of our science and technology personnel" but "have also enhanced the friendship and mutual understanding between our two peoples."[27] While these may be clichés, they are also a true reflection of the importance most Chinese leaders assign to scholarly exchanges. A different perspective—one not usually heard from government officials—was expressed by a Shanghai engineer:

> A Chinese is always Chinese. Blood is thicker than water. Those who have gone abroad are bound to come home as our country becomes stronger and more prosperous. And those who do not come back for various reasons will also make a contribution to China's modernization by furthering contacts and friendship between the Chinese people and those of other lands.[28]

---

[27] *China Business Review,* No. 4, July–August 1987, p. 13.

[28] Zhu Yuchao, "The Rage to Study Abroad," *China Reconstructs,* No. 12, December 1986, p. 49.

THE INTERNATIONAL PERSPECTIVE

It seems only appropriate to end this discussion by placing China's brain-drain problem into a broader, international perspective.

It is not uncommon for people whose experience with academic exchanges has been limited to post-1978 China to consider that country's problems to be different and "special." Such a perception is not altogether unwarranted. After all, China is the first communist country to train its successor generation in the West. Following 30 years of belligerency and isolation, suddenly to find so many Chinese students and scholars in U.S. universities was indeed phenomenal. Obvious questions arose. What were the effects of the Cultural Revolution on their scholastic background? Did they have the ability to compete in U.S. universities? How would they adapt to the very different environment? Could they communicate and get along with both faculty and students? Because of these special considerations, not only was the intimate involvement of the two governments unlike any previously experienced, but also large numbers of both professionals and well-wishers became involved in the late 1970s and early 1980s to smooth the way for Chinese students. However, the differences between Chinese and other foreign students stop at the brain-drain issue.

The "flight of intellectual capital" has been of great concern to all developing countries, especially since those individuals who tend to remain abroad are precisely the ones with the greatest initiative and enterprise—the ones who could make the greatest contribution to their home country. Compounding the problem is the universality of scientific and technical personnel. In their specialties any language handicap is minimized, and it is these critical people who are the most likely to stay abroad. It is not surprising, then, that this brain drain has been studied by many scholars and from many viewpoints. The similarities among all foreign students become very clear when we consider the consensus in these studies with regard to two aspects: what are some of the considerations for remaining abroad and what seem to be the most effective measures to assure return.

One of the more comprehensive studies on the brain-drain subject was done by the United Nations Institute for Training and Research (UNITAR).[29] It consisted of a survey of 6,500 student "stay-ons"

---

[29] William A. Glaser, *The Brain Drain: Emigration and Return* (New York: Pergamon Press, 1978).

in the United States and France from Argentina, Brazil, Colombia, Ghana, Greece, India, South Korea, and Sri Lanka. As we tick off the major findings of this study, the reader should have no difficulty in determining the points that are shared by Chinese students and scholars.

• Most students from developing countries plan to return home. Many of those who remain abroad to work do so for important practical experience and plan to return eventually.

• Most likely to stay abroad are those who studied some highly specialized field and believe that their new talents would be wasted at home. For example, one Tunisian professor who declined an invitation to join the staff of the Pasteur Institute in Tunis and instead took a position with the same institute in Paris expressed the view of many scientists: "I don't need a villa or a chauffeur-driven car. What I do require is a well-equipped laboratory in a stimulating university environment."[30]

• Specialists with highest rates of emigration share the same grievances: (a) feel isolated from newest developments in their fields; (b) jobs involve too much burdensome teaching and administration and too little research; or (c) poor facilities and equipment. In other words, job satisfaction is more important than salary.

• Although no clear-cut relation exists between ability and migration, persons with the lowest grades tend to return.

• Most common factors influencing return are family, friends, and patriotic feelings. Having children at home is one of the most important considerations in the decision to remain or return.

• The greater the association with nationals from the country of study and the lower the association with fellow students from home, the greater the tendency to emigrate. Visits home do not increase rate of return.

• Some decide to stay abroad until the job market improves at home or the government changes. Many return 10 to 15 years later to play an important role in their home country.

• And, perhaps the most important similarity shared with Chinese students, those with scholarships or special grants are more likely to return than those who study abroad privately. In other words, grants from government or employers in one's home country

---

[30]Moncef Mahroug, "Too Many Scholars, Not Enough Jobs," *IDRC Reports*, Vol. 17, No. 1, January 1988, p. 16.

are associated with return, and grants from universities abroad are associated with emigration. Furthermore, individuals who have jobs waiting are much more likely to return than those not yet employed when they went abroad.

The striking similarities between the brain-drain issues of Chinese students in the United States in the 1980s and those of students from other countries over the past several decades may surprise even the Chinese officials contemplating the dilemma. Solutions to the problem suggested by observers elsewhere also are similar to many of those introduced by the Chinese. Let us consider some of the suggested ways to control the emigration of professionals:

- The most frequently offered and the most obvious advice is also the most difficult for developing countries to implement: "create a climate for attracting and retaining talent." More specifically, improve both the living and working conditions of professionals and make it possible for talented professionals "to shine and grow in their jobs."[31]
- Limit education abroad to older students, to more advanced levels, to shorter periods of time, and to persons who have made a career start at home.[32]
- "Lack of careful co-ordination between development needs and student training abroad partly explains why education of these students in developed countries has turned into a broad avenue for permanent migration. . . ."[33]

With regard to Chinese students and scholars, there are other factors as well, but as we have already seen, Beijing has gradually (and probably independently) reached many of the above conclusions, incorporating virtually all of the proposed suggestions into current policies. How successful China will be in controlling the loss of brain power will depend on many factors, not the least of which is the economic progress and political mood in China—as perceived

---

[31]S. K. Chopra, ed., *Brain Drain and How to Reverse It* (New Delhi: Lancer International, 1986), p. 57.

[32]Charles P. Kindleberger, "Study Abroad and Emigration," in *The Brain Drain*, Walter Adams, ed. (New York: Macmillan, 1968), p. 135.

[33]Gregory Henderson, *Emigration of Highly-Skilled Manpower from Developing Countries* (New York: United Nations Institute for Training and Research, 1970), p. 68.

by the students. But, if the past has any bearing on the future, Beijing might keep two points in mind. First, the defections may not be forever and, second, certain advantages may still accrue to China even from those scholars who continue to live and work abroad. If the Chinese accept these as valid considerations, then the brain-drain issue may lose some of its immediate gravity.

3
Problems in Utilizing Returning Students and Scholars

Beijing is well aware that foreign training is the quickest way to improve the levels of scientific and technical knowledge while conserving investment. Moreover, while China may not always be able or willing to import the most advanced technologies, returning scholars bring with them the intellectual resources needed to create state-of-the-art technologies at home. But despite the recognized value of returning scholars to the nation, the problems associated with their placement and utilization have so far received much more publicity than their contributions—another example of how open and self-critical China is today. So, while we know that all too often these highly trained individuals have not been properly placed or fully utilized, there remains much that we do not know: What impact do returned students make on their work unit and on China's modernization in general? What role do they play in the diffusion of the knowledge that they gained abroad? How do the roles of foreign-trained specialists differ among universities, research institutes, and production-related enterprises? These and scores of other questions are of vital interest to people in the United States: to government agencies involved in exchange programs, to universities that have trained these individuals, and to anyone concerned with China's economic development and U.S.–China relations in general. At this juncture the answers are at best preliminary and at worst premature.

It may be the turn of the century before the importance and influence of the returning scholars will be fully understood and appreciated.

Obviously, the Chinese government has also been keenly interested in the impact of returning scholars on the economy, as well as in all other issues associated with the returnees. In China, too, the answers have been slow in coming—primarily for two reasons. First, significant numbers of younger students and scholars started to return to China only in the mid-1980s and, since this was innovational, the utilization of these individuals was haphazard. Time and experience were needed to identify the problems and attempt to correct them.

The second reason for the lack of answers is that the national organizations responsible for the assignment and management of professional personnel are still struggling with the pervasive problem of efficiently utilizing graduates from China's own institutions of higher education—experimenting with new ways of assigning specialists and, at the same time, attempting to introduce mobility into the employment system. If China's leaders are to avoid exacerbating the tensions between graduates of domestic universities and those returning from abroad, they must solve the utilization problem for both groups concomitantly.

With an ever-growing number of students returning from abroad and an increased awareness of their problems, in the last year or two, the Chinese government and some individual universities have initiated surveys to study both the contributions and the attitudes of recently returned students and scholars. The State Education Commission, for example, has provided some funding to a professor at Nankai University to conduct such a study, and the Chinese Academy of Sciences and the State Science and Technology Commission have initiated some preliminary surveys of their own.[1] Since Chinese officials appear to be quite open about sharing this information, it is reasonable to expect that in the next few years much more information will be available on the role of returning students and scholars.

The similarity of the employment complaints of graduates from

---

[1]From draft notes by Mary B. Bullock on her September 1987 meetings in Beijing with officials from personnel bureaus of the Chinese Academy of Sciences, the State Science and Technology Commission, and the State Education Commission. In 1988 the CSCPRC, in collaboration with several Chinese universities, initiated some preliminary surveys, on returning students and scholars.

both Chinese and foreign universities makes it important to understand at least some of the basic problems associated with the existing employment system—most specifically, the problems of job assignment and job mobility.[2]

CHINA'S SYSTEM OF JOB ASSIGNMENTS AND JOB MOBILITY

The inefficiency of planned economies is perhaps most clearly illustrated in the area of professional manpower. Planners must decide how many students will be accepted by institutions of higher education and how many will be enrolled in each major and its subfields. These decisions are made by anticipating the needs of the economy in years to come. With all its statistical resources, the United States decided some years ago that projecting work force needs into the future was a futile exercise. For a huge, developing country such as China the task is impossible, and for years there have been complaints about shortages, overages, and waste of the scarce manpower through the misassignment of graduates who, of course, had little or no say about their employment.

By the early 1980s, China's more progressive leaders were convinced that the country could no longer afford the extravagance of irrelevant job assignments. However, experimental reforms, which would eliminate the system of job assignments and institute procedures to allow some graduates freedom to choose employment and permit the enterprises some discretion about whom they would hire, quickly ran into difficulties including opposition from a large segment of the bureaucracy. The most serious drawback was that, nationwide, the supply of professionals, and especially of scientific and technical manpower, was well below the demand. This made it extremely difficult to assure a rational regional and sectoral distribution of college graduates, especially since the overwhelming majority of the graduates, if they exercised personal choice, would opt for employment in the large municipalities of China's coastal provinces.

The shortage of professionals in science and technology has had another unfortunate consequence. Employers who did not obtain

---

[2]For a detailed discussion of these and related issues, see Leo A. Orleans, "Reforms and Innovations in the Utilization of China's Scientific and Engineering Talent," in Denis F. Simon and Merle Goldman, eds., *Science and Technology in Post-Mao China* (Cambridge, Mass.: Council on East Asian Studies Publications, Harvard University Press, forthcoming).

their quota of college graduates were likely to resort to "back door" tactics to lure these individuals. There have been numerous instances of enterprises enticing specialists by offering them higher salaries, better housing, and other incentives. How to deal with these and related problems has stymied those responsible for reforms in personnel management. So far the results have been shifting policies and indecision, and the goal of balancing the desires of college graduates—whether with domestic or foreign degrees—with the needs of the country will take considerably more time.

Once assigned to an enterprise or an institution, a graduate was owned by it—in a very literal sense. The work unit, or *danwei,* provided not only a job, but also housing, medical care, additional education (when necessary), schooling for children, and numerous other amenities. The assignment was for life, and although, theoretically, an employee could change jobs with the approval of the *danwei,* the notion was so far-fetched that it was never an issue.

In the post-Mao period the "indenture" of professionals to a single work unit was recognized as an impediment to modernization. In the words of Lu Jiaxi, the former President of the Chinese Academy of Sciences, "Scientific and technological communities suffer from a lack of mobility, a condition not suited to modernization . . . [but] conducive to mental ossification, conservatism, and bureaucratism."[3] Nevertheless, the seeming unanimity in Beijing that mobility should be increased ran into a most formidable opponent: the *danwei.* Proclamations, directives, and arguments did little to influence the management cadres of either large or small enterprises and institutions to release their professionals to their competitors. The *danwei* has little interest in the general demand for or efficient utilization of the talents of these individuals, and there are numerous reports of unused specialists unable to change to another unit where their know-how is sorely needed. And, of course, the more valuable the employee, the less likely he or she will get permission to leave the unit. The government, persistently berating the practice of "hoarding scientific and technical personnel," has been actively innovative in trying to facilitate job mobility. There are now Talent Exchange and Consultation Service Centers in many large cities; "personnel-exchange conferences" are organized for professional and technical personnel to meet with representatives of units seeking new employ-

---

[3]Xinhua, May 28, 1984; JPRS-CST-033, Oct. 24, 1984, p. 17.

ees; there are reports of somewhat mysterious "talent development banks"; and newspapers have been carrying advertisements by enterprises seeking specialists. Unfortunately, although some successes have been reported with regard to job transfers, most accounts tell of failures. Perhaps the most authoritative judgment was given in a Circular of the State Council in July 1986, which pointed out that despite some progress, the practice of "overstocking, wasting, and misusing scientists and technicians has not been fundamentally eliminated."

The discussion that follows touches on many of these issues as they relate to China's highest level of personnel—the students and scholars returning from abroad.

THE MOUNTING PROBLEMS

In the early 1980s, returning scholars were few in number and not a priority issue. The problems that were to arise were neither contemplated nor anticipated. Chinese authorities, in the process of expanding contacts with foreign universities and research institutions, were much more concerned about the candidate-selection process and a variety of other considerations associated with maximizing the number and quality of people sent abroad. Furthermore, since the earlier returnees were primarily older scholars selected by their units (usually institutes of the Chinese Academy of Sciences or one of the more prestigious universities) and returned to their own *danwei,* they managed to resume their research, assume responsible administrative positions, or perhaps do both. In fact, almost all the success stories were and continue to be from these influential institutions.

A study by Otto Schnepp, former science attaché at the U.S. Embassy in Beijing, showed considerable success in the reintegration of these scholars within the Chinese Academy of Sciences,[4] and there are many such reports from Chinese sources as well. For example, in 1984 *Guangming Ribao* reported that "the overwhelming majority of Chinese research institutes are paying great attention to the persons who have studied overseas . . . by creating the conditions necessary

---

[4] Otto Schnepp, University of Southern California, "The Chinese Exchange Scholar Program in Science and Engineering," unpublished paper sponsored by the National Science Foundation.

for enhancing their newly developed skills" and that a significant number of them have been promoted.[5] Later that year came a report that returning students are "playing leading roles in teaching, scientific research, and research and development, according to education departments."[6] And again, specifically mentioned were the academies of sciences and social sciences and Shanghai Jiaotung and Qinghua universities. More recent successes are also reported from prestigious institutions such as the Chinese University of Science and Technology[7] and the Shanghai Institute of Organic Chemistry,[8] and from the National Defense Science, Technology, and Industry Commission[9]—all of which claim that they "cherish their returned students" and "give full play to their roles."

In other words, there have always been enough success stories to report or to include in a lead paragraph. In the last few years, however, the balance definitely shifted and many more stories began to deal with the critical and complex problems associated with the proper placement of returning scholars and researchers. First, the number of returnees started to increase and by 1984 it was reported at "some 10,000." Moreover, the composition of this group gradually began to change. The older and more established scholars who returned to their former work units gave way to the younger students with both undergraduate and graduate degrees, whose job assignments were not predestined and therefore subject to misassignment. Finally, and despite a few minor zigzags, China has been undergoing a liberalization process, and those who had been abroad returned to an atmosphere of increased expectations.

Given this setting, what are the specific complaints of the returning students and scholars? Scores of articles have discussed these issues and a number of surveys on the subject have been taken by both the national and provincial governments and institutions. The basic complaints fall into some well-defined categories and are summarized below.[10]

[5] *GMRB*, Sept. 23, 1984; JPRS-CPS-84-090, Dec. 12, 1984, p. 51.

[6] Xinhua, Dec. 2, 1984; FBIS, Dec. 3, 1984, p. K6.

[7] *Renmin Ribao* (*People's Daily*), March 26, 1986; JPRS-CST-86-020, p. 11.

[8] *Jiefang Ribao* (*Liberation Daily*), Nov. 18, 1985; JPRS-CST-86-005, Feb. 2, 1986, p. 9.

[9] *GMRB*, Sept. 17, 1985; JPRS-CST-85-038, Nov. 5, 1985, p. 1.

[10] This summary is based, in part, on the following sources: *Kexuexue Yu Kexue Jishu Guanli* (hereafter referred to as *KYKJG*) (*Science of Science and Management of Science and Technology*), No. 11, Nov. 12, 1985; JPRS-CST-86-008, March 1, 1986, pp. 1–5. *KYKJG*, No. 11, Nov. 12, 1984; JPRS-CST-85-027, pp.

There are the predictable complaints about cadres—both managers and administrators. Charges are that they lack understanding of the roles of returned personnel and "arrange for employment" without any regard to an individual's talent, specialty, or experience. A universally familiar grievance is that promotions take people out of research and educational activities and into administration. Although this may seem especially wasteful when it happens to foreign-trained scientific and technical personnel, there are, of course, important pluses, in the long term, for the management of scientific institutions. There is also the inevitable prejudice against young people, who rarely get promoted, no matter what their professional competence. This wasteful cultural bias will take many years to overcome. Cadres continue to have a "leftist bias toward intellectuals," convinced that anyone who spends any length of time abroad is "subjected to several bad influences" or becomes "a political blank."

According to one Chinese survey, about one-fifth of the returnees cannot use the specializations and knowledge that they acquired abroad because of improper job-assignment, for which the cadres are also held responsible. This is said to be a higher proportion than for graduates of Chinese universities—a contention that might reasonably be disputed by citing innumerable reports concerning the irrational assignment of domestic graduates. Moreover, the returnees find it difficult to make a positive contribution since they are not allowed the independence of making their own decisions with regard to research topics. What is especially upsetting to some is that while they were abroad, their research topics were taken over by their colleagues. This is a curious complaint that may refer more to lost opportunities for promotion rather than to specific research topics.

In addition to improper assignment, foreign-trained scholars deplore the inadequate laboratory facilities, a shortage of equipment and capital for scientific research, and generally poor working conditions. These problems were stressed at the 1984 conference on sending students abroad, when State Councilor Zhang Jingfu admitted that "70 percent of returning students are not being fully used

---

24-32. *GMRB,* Nov. 24, 1984; JPRS-CST-85-005, Feb. 20, 1985, pp. 10–11; also in *CD*, Nov. 25, 1984. *CD*, Nov. 30, 1984; Xinhua, Nov. 29, 1984; FBIS, Nov. 30, 1984, p. K7. *GMRB,* Sept. 17, 1985; JPRS-CST-85-038, Nov. 5, 1985, p. 1. Xinhua, Dec. 2, 1984; FBIS, Dec. 3, 1984, p. K6. *Jiefang Ribao,* Nov. 18, 1985; JPRS-CST-86-005, Feb. 11, 1986, p. 9.

because of a shortage of advanced facilities and unsuitable work assignments." At the same time, many organizations are accused of
wasting large sums of money by importing useless instruments and
supplies, and then discovering that there are no funds to purchase
equipment urgently needed to carry out planned research.

Still other miscellaneous but professionally related issues upset
the returned scholars. Foreign-trained scholars say that they want
guaranteed time for research, claiming that too much of their time is
spent on activities that could be performed by assistants and other
support personnel. They also would like to get reimbursed for their
professional expenditures. They demand a solution to the "problem
of knowledge renewal," without which they "will die academically."
Most scholars, especially those located outside of Beijing, Shanghai,
and Guangzhou, feel cut off from foreign contacts, and all seem
to want more frequent exchanges with their counterparts in foreign
countries.

Not to detract from their importance, the most universal complaints are also of the more mundane variety, such as low wages,
inadequate housing, and "worries and trouble at home." According
to one survey conducted in 22 institutions of higher education and
14 research and development units in Shenyang, 80 percent of the
returned scholars receive less than 100 yuan, and 45 percent, less
than 80 yuan per month. Of 10 individuals with doctoral degrees
from abroad, 6 earn only 78 yuan a month and are referred to as
the "78-yuan doctors."[11] There are few bonuses given and most returned scholars consider themselves to be in the "poor household"
category. The low salaries in this example are especially striking
because Shenyang is a highly industrialized city in one of China's
richest provinces. The most likely explanation for the low compensation was alluded to above: A large proportion of the returnees are
young (especially by Chinese standards), and no matter how much
they try to change the tradition, for the most part age and seniority
are more important in determining salary than qualifications and

---

[11] Beijing has been experimenting with the difficult task of wage reforms
since the early 1980s and several formulas are now being tested. To place
these salaries in context, the average monthly wage (includes base pay, bonuses,
seniority pay, and other components) for workers and employees is about
100 yuan ("Last Year China's Force of Staff and Workers Grew and Wages
Increased," *Gongren Ribao* [*Worker's Daily*], Feb. 9, 1987; JPRS-CEA-87-043,
May 19, 1987, p. 110). A mid-career urban high school teacher also gets about
100 yuan a month.

job descriptions. One Chinese journal cites the embarrassing (and highly questionable) statement that only Kampuchea has lower pay and worse conditions for intellectuals than China.[12]

The problem of housing, of course, is not limited to foreign-educated scholars—it is a national problem. Although some of the more prominent institutions are likely to provide comparatively decent housing, most do not, and the living conditions of their professionals are indeed inadequate. To refer again to the Shenyang survey, some 90 percent of the interviewed scholars are over 36 years of age, most with children and many with older parents in their household, and yet about one-third of them live in only one room, while half live in two rooms.

Another frustration for foreign-trained scholars, especially the more prominent ones with substantial scholarly achievements, is that their titles do not properly reflect their positions. According to these individuals, it is not simply a matter of ego; they feel that inappropriate titles have affected their academic exchanges both within China and with foreign countries and have limited their influence with graduate students. Within Chinese culture this complaint may not be as frivolous as it seems.

THE LEGITIMACY OF THE COMPLAINTS

Before proceeding to some of the suggested solutions to the problems raised by the returning scholars, it may be worth speculating about the legitimacy of their complaints. No one can deny the problems. Laboratories, equipment, and facilities obviously do not compare with those in the United States and other advanced nations; salaries and living conditions are not what one might expect for that segment of society so vital to China's modernization; and indeed there are many instances of misassignment that negate the main purpose of foreign education, not to mention the wasted expenditure. But consider the similarity of complaints expressed by domestically trained Chinese scientists and technicians in a recent sample survey taken by the Scientific and Technological Association of Hunan Province.[13]More than half of the 1,679 people surveyed complained about their inability to make their own decisions, the bureaucratic working style of their leaders who did not make good

---

[12]*Shijie Jingji Daobao (World Economic Herald)*, Nov. 24, 1986; FBIS, Dec. 19, 1986, p. K13.

[13] *BR*, No. 10, March 9, 1987, p. 27.

use of their talents, the burden of their household chores, and the fact that their incomes were lower than those of physical laborers of the same age. Just under half the sample said that their research instruments and data were behind the times, the quality of logistics was poor, and the shortage of housing was serious. Of necessity, scholars returning from abroad must work within the same milieu.

Further, consider the similarities of complaints expressed by U.S.-educated students returning to Taiwan. According to recent surveys, the first wish of most returned students is to teach at a college or university, but wherever they end up, most say they have "always been dissatisfied" with "opportunities for advancement and learning new skills, salaries, and research equipment." As for the employers in Taiwan, in general they appreciate the qualifications of foreign-trained students, but they also have complaints that are undoubtedly similar to those felt in China. Foreign-educated graduates in Taiwan were criticized for their emphasis on theory over practice—something they had little control over; some employers said that "the feeling of individualism in the returning students was too strong"; and a "small number" of answers to surveys "focused on the superiority complex of returning students, their tendency to switch jobs, and their materialistic attitudes." [14]

To take the role of "devil's advocate" a step further, let us look at the aforementioned complaints from the perspective of the faculty of an imaginary U.S. institution of higher education or, for that matter, of most professionals in a large bureaucracy. Is it not commonplace to hear colleagues complain about underutilization of their talents and expenditure of too much of their time on "routine work" at the expense of creative endeavors? Sexual, racial, political, or religious discrimination certainly exists in China, but such charges can and are easily made about academic personnel practices elsewhere. Inappropriate assignment is a less pressing problem in a country where free choice in job selection is a given, but in China, where virtually everyone would like to join an institute of one of the science academies or a key university in a major eastern city, any other assignment would, by definition, be considered inappropriate. Complaints about inadequate research funds and the need for more up-to-date equipment and the ever-elusive research assistants are so universal that they require no comment. There may be some basis

---

[14] *Chinese-English Bilingual Monthly,* Vol. 11, No. 5, May 1986, pp. 6–17.

to the returned scholar's lament about being unable to keep up with the latest foreign developments in science and technology but, on the other hand, there is certainly no shortage of the latest foreign literature in the institutions to which a foreign-trained scholar is likely to be assigned. Inappropriately low wages is indeed a legitimate complaint, but also one that is not unknown in the United States, especially among educators and research scientists.

The above parallel, cynical as it may seem, is not intended to belabor the universality of youthful bravado and unrealistic expectations but rather to suggest that many of the problems go beyond systemic inefficiencies. In other words, while China's problems with returned students are indeed serious, they are not unique, and we therefore should not ignore the possibility that some human factors are also at play. It is very possible that a student or scholar spending several years abroad becomes not so much "spiritually polluted" as simply spoiled.[15] Most important, it would seem that many students return to China with exaggerated evaluations of their own worth, as well as unrealistic expectations of what China can provide and what China expects. Not to underestimate the unique problems of returnees, it is important to repeat that the complaints voiced by returning students are essentially identical to those expressed by the graduates of Chinese universities—not of the two- or three-year specialized colleges, but of the elite universities.[16]

There is also a flip side to this situation. Many graduates with a fresh degree from a foreign university go home with great trepidation because expectations of them are so high. This problem is probably less obvious in the sciences than in such fields as engineering. In the United States, for example, engineering graduates with a master's degree are likely to start their career at the bottom of the professional rung and gradually work their way up through experience. When

---

[15]In fact, Chinese educators complain that the new breeds of college students are already spoiled when they come to the university. As children, they traveled the road of "key elementary school–key middle school–university," with the "entire family machinery turning around them as axle centers." Escorted to the university by the head of household, many students had never done any housework, and there was much concern about their ability to manage both studies and chores by themselves (Yang Xinyuan, "A Spoiled Generation and Perplexed Parents," Zhejiang Ribao [Zhejiang Daily], Oct. 24, 1986; JPRS-CPS-87-007, Feb. 9, 1987).

[16]See, for example, "Young S&T Personnel Hope to Solve Four Problems," GMRB, July 10, 1986; JPRS-CST-86-046, Nov. 5, 1986, p. 22.

Chinese graduates with the same degree return from abroad, great things are expected of them immediately, simply by virtue of their foreign education. Usually, however, they do not yet know how to translate their book knowledge into solving the practical everyday problems of their enterprise. For some, spending a few years in a U.S. factory may be more useful in the long run than a sheepskin. It is this belated realization that is behind current efforts to emphasize the need for students studying abroad to acquire practical experience along with book-learning.

SOME PROPOSED SOLUTIONS

Whether the problems listed by returning students and scholars are taken at face value, or viewed in a slightly modified form, they no doubt are of great concern to Beijing, not only because of the drag they produce on reaching the goals of modernization, but also because students who are still abroad pay close attention to the conditions they will be facing on their return. And yet the solutions being proposed to correct "inferior working conditions and low management levels" rely on familiar and sometimes unrealistic prescriptions.[17] It is reasonable, for example, to call on leaders to have a better appreciation of the important role of returned intellectuals, to show political trust, and to strive to create conditions that will maximize the performance of the specialists. It is also reasonable to expect that individuals returning from abroad will be properly placed and should be able to change jobs and not be held back by some illegitimate pretext. On the other hand, the remedy that calls for research funds (including foreign-exchange funds) to be under the control of those actually performing scientific research is no more realistic in China than in any Western nation, where basic resource allocation continues to be essentially a political decision. Other suggestions for improving the conditions for returnees may be difficult, but manageable. Scholars should be encouraged to develop cooperative linkages with their counterparts in foreign countries; they should be released from the "tedious formalities of administrative activities"; they should receive appropriate compensation; and they should be able to have research assistants of their choosing.

---

[17]See, for example, *KYKJG*, No. 11, Nov. 12, 1985; JPRS-CST-86-008, March 1, 1986, pp. 4–5.

Although most of the suggested solutions to the complaints of the returnees are predictable, there have also been some interesting innovations. For example, one step to improve the placement of returning scholars was announced in 1984 by State Councilor Zhang Jingfu, who stated quite positively, not only that "every student returning from abroad should have the right to choose his work and work unit," but also that "the State would allocate 20 million yuan [US$8 million] to set up 10 places throughout the country where returned students would have equipment to work with while they spend two years seeking suitable jobs."[18] By mid-1987 the number of "temporary holding centers" is said to have increased to over 100, located in 20 cities. They are primarily established for returning scientists and function as way stations in the scholar's search for work or suitable research opportunities. It is presumed that some domestically trained PhDs may also take advantage of these holding centers. If the applicant passes an entrance examination, he or she will be able to remain at the center for two years doing research while looking for work and, if necessary, get another two-year extension. The research fellow would also receive an annual stipend from the government.

Some returnees with advanced degrees in the sciences may also be placed in one of the "open research laboratories," which were first announced in August 1985 and whose number is rapidly growing. These independently funded up-to-date laboratories are affiliated with institutes of the Chinese Academy of Sciences and several universities, but have independent state funding. One of the main functions of these modern laboratories is to assemble groups of top scientists from universities and research institutes of the Chinese Academy of Sciences to work for a given period of time on specific priority projects in an environment conducive to productive research. This may not solve the problem of the individual's research interests, but it is another way to link research with production—one of China's immediate priorities. In some obscure way the open laboratories are also said to "promote the mobility of scientific and technical personnel." In August 1986, of a total staff of 1,318 scientific and technical personnel in 19 open research laboratories, less than one-quarter were permanently assigned to the laboratories, while the rest were "guest scientists." They are expected to return to their work unit

---

[18] *CD*, Nov. 11, 1984, p. 3.

when the project is over. In addition to accommodating some of
the most prominent Chinese scientists, open laboratories also invite
foreign scholars (26 in 1986) to lecture and do cooperative research.
The open research laboratories are also said to provide a temporary
workplace for returning Chinese PhDs in the sciences while a decision is made as to where their knowledge might be best utilized.[19]
Just how this works in practice is not entirely clear. Since institutions that paid to send a student or scholar abroad would be most
unlikely voluntarily to release this individual to work in an open laboratory, these facilities probably accommodate young scholars not
assigned to a *danwei* prior to foreign study. Furthermore, despite
the modern research facilities, not all the returning students look at
open research laboratories with favor: according to one U.S. official
in China, some returned Chinese PhDs are suspicious of the open
laboratories, claiming that their main function is to maintain close
control over the returning scholars.

By way of a summary, let us consider a commentary by a Chinese
academic who accurately reflects both the problems and the possible
solutions as perceived by the Chinese and as reflected in many of the
recent policy changes with regard to sending students and scholars
abroad.[20] Shen Xiaodan looks at returnees not from the perspective
of the individual, but from the perspective of China's economic
needs, and in that sense he is echoing some frequent complaints
heard in other developing countries. Mainly, he deplores the fact
that "there has not been a complete, long-range study of going
abroad for study" and that the program was "not coordinated with
local and national scientific and technical needs or its compatibility
with China's economic needs."

In discussing the defection of specialists trained abroad, Shen
points out that the likelihood of such an eventuality is increased by
host countries that encourage students in scarce disciplines to remain. To support this contention, he cites what must be tenuous

---

[19]"Address to the Second Work Conference on Open Research Laboratories
in the Chinese Academy of Sciences," an unpublished paper by Zhou Guangzhao,
President of the Chinese Academy of Sciences; and a telephone conversation
with Dr. Ray Wu, Biochemistry Section, Department of Molecular and Cell
Biology, Cornell University.

[20]Shen Xiaodan, "A Study of China's Policy of Importing Brainpower
Viewed from the Angle of Economic Development," *KYKJG*, No. 11, Nov. 12,
1984; JPRS-CST-85-027, Aug. 22, 1985.

statistics. Between 1961 and 1972, according to Shen's data, the United States, Great Britain, and Canada provided US$46 billion in aid to developing countries, but by training professionals from these countries and absorbing them into their own labor forces, they gained capital valued at US$51 billion. In fact, he believes that advanced countries tend to attract the best and most needed scientific and technical personnel from developing nations, while "pushing out manpower they have no need for." This notion, shared by many Chinese officials, may have some validity, but it is also usually misunderstood. While it is true that the best scholars are more likely to remain abroad, it is important to understand that this is not due to a national policy, at least in the case of the United States, but rather a process of "natural selection" by institutions of higher education and enterprises over which the U.S. government has little if any control.

Another national concern discussed by Shen is that too many students abroad are not majoring in fields important to the development of China's science and technology. Contrary to a recent article in *Renmin Ribao*, which noted that "we must make proper arrangements for the work of returned students in accordance with the principle of applying what they have learned,"[21] Shen reflects the more prevalent belief (now incorporated into policy) that the priorities should be reversed and that students must learn what the country needs. Between 70 and 80 percent of the students have chosen basic or applied subjects as majors, making it difficult to raise the professional level of scientific and technical personnel engaged in production technology and developmental research. Given China's level of development, even with the best of intentions, she cannot possibly provide up-to-date facilities and equipment, not to mention meaningful research projects, to the thousands of physicists, chemists, and other physical scientists now getting graduate degrees in the United States. The situation is made worse by the fact that domestic universities are also accused of training too many high-level specialists, which, according to He Dongchang, Vice-Minister of the State Education Commission, "is not in conformity with China's economic development in the primary stage of socialism."[22]

---

[21] *Renmin Ribao (People's Daily)*, July 13, 1986; FBIS, July 17, 1986, p. K7.

[22] Xinhua, Oct. 29, 1987; FBIS-CHI-87-210, Oct. 30, 1987, p. 22. Conversely, the demand for graduates in foreign languages (especially English), accounting, and computer science is said to be 5 to 10 times greater than their actual numbers (*CD*, "College Graduate Shortage Eased," Oct. 17, 1987, p. 3).

Given China's level of development, the consequences are predictable: While there is often a surplus of research scholars in some of the basic sciences, creating an even more serious shortage of up-to-date equipment and laboratories, there is at the same time a serious shortage of personnel in production-related research, where there often is an adequate supply of equipment, instruments, and materials. Shen presumably would disagree with a compromise offered in a 1984 *Guangming Ribao* editorial reminding the leadership of units that the creative strength of the returnees should be rationally employed, but that "their professional directions can be adjusted slightly in light of China's specific realities and conditions. . . ."[23] He would insist that all "adjustments" should be made prior to sending scholars abroad, and indeed, the Chinese are now actively discouraging their students from getting U.S. degrees in theoretical sciences, while encouraging more degrees in engineering and other applied fields.

Although Shen's article discusses foreign education, his basic solution seems to focus primarily on practices that have already become fairly standard in China's commercial dealings with corporations from industrially advanced nations. He believes that knowledge and know-how must be imported with the products China buys abroad. In other words, as part of the plant-and-equipment package, foreign firms must contract to train specialists—presumably either abroad or in China. This, of course, is already the case, and over the years thousands of Chinese workers have been trained in the United States. Both Chinese and U.S. partners to contractual arrangements and joint ventures find that the technical and managerial skills gained by spending from several weeks to over a year in training by a U.S. company brings useful returns.[24]

Finally, Shen believes that the importation of manpower and its rational utilization cannot depend on "patching together a few policies," but must be the responsibility of some (unspecified) unified

---

[23] *GMRB*, Aug. 29, 1984; JPRS-CST-85-003, Jan. 28, 1985, p. 23.

[24] For an excellent discussion of these training programs, see Julia S. Sensenbrenner, "The Training Component," *The China Business Review*, November–December 1986, pp. 8–12. In 1984 the following number of visas were issued to Chinese workers and employees: 284 H-1s (workers of distinguished merit and ability), 196 H-2s (other temporary workers), 44 H-3s (industrial trainees), and 251 L-1s (intercompany transfers, usually limited to joint venture partners) (*1984 Statistical Yearbook of the Immigration and Naturalization Service* [Washington, D.C.: U.S. Department of Justice]).

management, which will also have some responsibility for the acquisition of hardware. He considers these to be vital prerequisites for reaching China's economic goals. In the sense that the State Education Commission now has primary responsibility for overseeing all foreign education, at least half of Shen's objective is implemented; uniting this responsibility with the acquisition of hardware, however, does not appear to be even on the horizon.

The problems associated with job assignments for returning students and scholars are, of course, well known to Beijing. But given the country's level of development, and with the best of intentions, it is impossible to provide up-to-date equipment, not to mention meaningful research projects, to the thousands of physicists, chemists, and other physical scientists now getting graduate degrees abroad. Many of the problems mentioned above would indeed be eased with the establishment of more direct ties between foreign study and domestic needs and priorities, and, if implemented, the June 1987 State Education Commission regulations on foreign study should go far in doing that. If, as now stipulated, the State Education Commission will indeed set quotas by field of study there will be more symmetry between training and China's need; and if the personnel going abroad on government programs sign agreements with their units, stipulating objectives, subjects to be studied, length of required service at home after studying abroad, rights, responsibilities, and so on, then at least the initial assignment will presumably be settled. From the Western perspective, however, any interference with free choice in academic matters is anathema and just how the Chinese students will react to these new conditions is also still open to speculation.

Part II

Chinese Students and Scholars in the United States: Numbers and Characteristics

4

Understanding the Statistics:
Problems and Issues

As mentioned in the Preface, ever since the exchanges started in 1978, the figure for the total number of Chinese students and scholars in the United States has eluded officials on both sides of the Pacific. Because, on the face of it, this basic figure should not be so difficult to determine, its absence inevitably draws first surprise, then disbelief. Surely either the United States with its advanced computers or China with her presumed controls over people should have the answer. It is just this incredulity that prompts the inclusion in the body of this report, rather than in an appendix, a detailed discussion of the problems and issues associated with statistics on Chinese students in the United States. Many readers will undoubtedly want to understand some of the methodological and institutional problems that have been responsible for this void; others, who are not interested in the hows and whys of the data, can skip directly to the statistical tables and the analysis in the sections that follow.

CHINESE STATISTICS ON SENDING STUDENTS ABROAD

Although China's notoriously poor statistics (in all fields) have improved dramatically in the 1980s, there are still many deficiencies to overcome. Among them are a shortage of personnel trained in statistics and a traditional casualness with regard to numbers—a *cha-bu-duo* attitude which, despite the purported accuracy of the 1982 national census, has been especially evident when it comes to "people numbers."[1]

The problems associated with keeping track of the movement of students and scholars in and out of China are magnified by the number of institutions, scattered throughout the country, involved in the process. Not only are student exit permits issued by various ministries, bureaus, universities, and institutes, but even passports are obtained in scattered administrative jurisdictions, with officially sponsored scholars getting them from the Ministry of Foreign Affairs and privately sponsored students getting their passports from the Public Security Bureaus. As is so often the case in China, a particular locality or administrative entity may have reasonably accurate figures, but the system breaks down in the process of transmission and aggregation, which, for the most part, is still done manually. Beijing has not published either an integrated series of year-by-year figures for students and scholars sent abroad or a breakdown by country of study. Most of the highly rounded figures reported by the Chinese refer to cumulative totals between 1978 and a given year, occasionally indicate distributions by country of study, sporadically show figures on returnees, and never include a total of students in any country in any particular year (see Table 4-1). How accurate are the available figures?

In 1986 (apparently for the first time) China published a set of figures under the heading "number of students sent abroad." Although no explanation was provided, the figures are obviously too low to include either scholars or privately supported students, and since they were released by the State Education Commission, the numbers must refer only to the officially sponsored students. From this assumption we can then derive the distribution of government-sponsored students between the United States and other countries (see Table 4-2).

Although combining Chinese and U.S. statistics in one calculation is somewhat risky, since the Chinese rarely publish any breakdown of students and scholars by country of study, even an approximate distribution between the United States and the other 60-plus countries is of special interest. Although the results seem to contradict Chinese reports that two-thirds of all students and scholars

---

[1] See, for example, Leo A. Orleans, "China's Statistics: The Impossible Dream," *The American Statistician*, May 1974, pp. 47–52.

TABLE 4-1 PRC Students and Scholars Abroad (all countries)

| Between Jan. 1979 and | Number | | | Total Returned |
	Total	Official	Private	
Nov. 1979[a]	(2,230)	2,230	n.a.	--
End of 1979[b]	(2,700)	2,700	n.a.	--
End of 1980[c]	5,192	n.a.	n.a.	--
Mid-1982[d]	(12,000)	12,000	n.a.	--
End of 1983[e]	25,500	18,500	7,000	(7,000)
June 1984[f]	33,000	26,000	7,000	14,000
Mid-1985[g]	36,800	29,000	7,800	15,000
End of 1985[h]	38,000	30,000	8,000	16,500
Mid-1987[i]	50,000	40,000	10,000	20,000

NOTE: Although figures for a number of years are missing, the totals that are reported appear in many sources. In most cases the starting date of January 1979 is clearly indicated; when the source indicates the end month, it is shown in the table; the more general time periods in the table were surmised from the date of the earliest publication in which the figure appeared. The totals in parentheses do not include the privately sponsored students.

SOURCES:
[a] Beijing Review (BR), p. 5, No. 47, 1979.
[b] Xinhua, Dec. 22, 1979; Foreign Broadcast Information Service (FBIS), Jan. 7, 1980, p. L6..
[c] Xinhua, Nov. 7, 1980; FBIS, Nov. 7, 1980, p. L32. This total includes 3,963 visiting scholars, 562 postgraduate students, and 667 undergraduates.
[d] Xinhua, Aug. 22, 1982; FBIS, Aug. 23, 1982, p. K15.
[e] BR, No. 3, Jan. 16, 1984, p. 11.
[f] Xinhua, Nov. 29, 1984; Joint Publications Research Service (JPRS)-CST-85, Jan. 3, 1985, p. 5.
[g] Banyuetan (Semi-Monthly Talks), Aug. 25, 1985; JPRS-CST-85-037, Oct. 29, 1985, p. 4.
[h] Xinhua, July 8, 1986; FBIS, July 9, 1986, p. K12.
[i] Xinhua, June 10, 1987; FBIS, June 15, 1987, p. K7.

come to the United States, the discrepancy can be explained by the fact that the figures in Table 4-2 apply only to officially sponsored students. If scholars and privately supported students were included, the proportion in the United States would undoubtedly come closer to two-thirds of the total numbers sent abroad. As for figures in Table 4-2, in the early postnormalization years, the majority of Chinese students were indeed sent to Europe and Japan, but in just three years the balance shifted, so that by 1983 most were coming to the United States. Since this country is the overwhelming choice of

TABLE 4-2 Estimated Percentage of Officially Sponsored Students
Sent to the United States

Year	Number of Students Sent Abroad[a]	Number of J-1 Visas Issued by the U.S.[b]	Number of Students Sent to Other Countries[c]	Percentage of Students Sent to U.S.[d]
1980	2,124	336	1,758	17
1981	2,922	680	2,242	23
1982	2,326	950	1,376	41
1983	2,633	1,572	1,061	60
1984	3,073	1,783	1,290	58
1985	4,888	2,507	2,381	51
1986	6,380	3,069	3,311	48

SOURCES:

[a]Achievement of Education in China, 1980-1985, State Education
Commission, Beijing, 1986, p. 50. The 1986 figure was reported
in PRC Yearbook 1987, p. 465.
[b]From Table 5-8.
[c]Subtracting column 2 from column 1.
[d]Percentage in column 2 of column 1.

Chinese students, the downturn in the proportion (not in absolute
numbers) coming to the United States in the last three years may
also seem somewhat surprising. One reason for this is that it is much
easier to obtain a visa for Canada and some of the European countries, where stricter immigration policies and stringent enforcement
also make their return much more certain than if they came to the
United States.

Until recently, Chinese diplomatic officials in the United States
readily admitted that they did not have an accurate count of the
numbers of scholars and students in this country, and such a number
rarely appeared in Chinese sources.[2] In 1986, however, with the help
of a newly acquired computer, the Chinese Embassy in Washington
began inputting data on all students and scholars with J-1 visas
in the United States, their locations, their majors, and probably

---

[2]When released, the number was likely to be picked up by numerous
publications. For example, the 1984 release stating that as of April 1984, 8,900
officially sponsored and 4,000 privately sponsored students had come to the
United States and 3,600 had already returned to China appeared in many
sources (see, for example, *CD*, April 28, 1984).

other pertinent information. This has obviously greatly improved the statistical base available to the Chinese officials, but they continue to lack one important set of figures. Although the information on those entering the United States is said to be reasonably accurate, the Embassy is not always informed when individuals return to China. What this means, of course, is that although China's capability of estimating the number of persons in the United States under official Chinese auspices is rapidly improving, it still must be viewed as an approximation. And, of course, Chinese figures on the number of returnees must be even more problematic. Moreover, since there is no attempt to keep track of the privately funded students, a formula for determining the total number of Chinese scholars and students in the United States remains unattainable.

In any case, according to statistics obtained from the Chinese Embassy, in November 1986 there were 4,987 scholars (46 percent), 5,716 graduate students (53 percent), and 116 undergraduate students (1 percent) in the United States, for a total of 10,819 scholars and students with J-1 visas. This total, as noted below, is several thousand lower than that derived from the U.S. Information Agency (USIA) data. While it is true that a discrepancy between U.S. and Chinese figures is inevitable, in this case, most of the difference can be explained by the fact that Chinese statistics exclude all visiting scholars who spend less than six months in the United States, a distinction which this country does not make but which has some merit.

Despite China's problems with statistics, after considering the difficulties on the U.S. side, it may not be too risky to suggest that in years to come, we may be looking to Chinese officials for the most accurate data on scholars and students in the United States.

Tangentially, it is interesting to consider the significant growth of foreign students in Chinese universities. According to the State Education Commission, their number has grown from 1,270 in 1979 to more than 6,000 in 1987 and is expected to reach almost 10,000 by the end of 1990. Just over half of all foreign students in China are said to come from 77 countries in the third world.[3]

---

[3] *CD*, Dec. 18, 1987, p. 1.

U.S. IMMIGRATION AND NATURALIZATION SERVICE
DATA ON CHINESE STUDENTS

As already mentioned, many people may find it especially difficult to understand how a country that is as statistically and techno-
logically sophisticated as the United States can also only guess about
the number of Chinese in U.S. institutions of higher education. It is
important to understand why. Two U.S. agencies control the entry
of foreign students and scholars and theoretically should be able to
provide statistics on their numbers: the Immigration and Naturalization Service (INS) and the Visa Office of the U.S. Department of
State.

The problem with U.S. immigration statistics produced by the
INS was carefully analyzed in a National Academy of Sciences 1985
report. Aptly subtitled "A Story of Neglect," it referred to immigration as "the Cinderella of the federal statistical system."[4] Indeed,
despite recent efforts to improve the management of immigration
statistics by introducing more advanced computer technology, the
INS is still unable to produce much of the data sought by government policymakers, as well as demographers and other scholars
specializing in the study of migration and immigration. Data on
the 20 nonimmigrant categories entering the country are said to be
especially difficult to collect and, according to one anonymous INS
spokesman, the figures on Chinese students are virtually useless. Let
us consider some of the specific reasons.

Anyone who consults the statistical yearbooks, published annually by the INS, is immediately taken aback by the figures in the table
entitled "Nonimmigrants Admitted by Country of Citizenship." The
1985 INS yearbook reports a total of 202,447 nonimmigrants admitted to the United States from China. This is obviously an impossible
figure, but there is fortunately a footnote (which, incidentally, did
not appear in previous years). The footnote reveals that the figures
under the "China" entry include both the People's Republic of China
and Taiwan! It also provides a breakdown between the two entities,
but not by analyzing INS data. It relies on information provided
by the Visa Office of the U.S. Department of State: "A total of approximately 143,000 visas were issued to these two countries in fiscal
year 1985: 93,000 to Taiwan and 50,000 to the Peoples' Republic

---

[4]Daniel B. Levine et al., eds., *Immigration Statistics* (Washington, D.C.:
National Academy Press, 1985).

of China." There is no clarification of the discrepancy between the 202,447 in the table and the 143,000 in the footnote, no distribution of the totals by specific categories of nonimmigrants, and no explanation for the need to rely on Department of State figures.[5]

Unquestionably, the INS has legitimate problems that are not easily overcome. At the time of entry, every nonimmigrant fills out Form I-94 in which the reason for entering the United States must be shown. In theory, therefore, the INS should have in its data base the number of PRC students (F-1 visas) and PRC "exchange visitors" (visiting scholars with J-1 visas, in our terminology) entering the country each year, and its Statistical Analysis Branch did, in fact, provide some figures. However, to anyone familiar with the flow of Chinese students and scholars to the United States it would be immediately evident that these figures were grossly inflated, especially for the F-1 category. Although some part of the excess could be the double-counting of multiple entries, in the case of students and scholars from China multiple trips between the two countries are relatively infrequent. In response to a request for a better explanation for the much lower figures reported by the Visa Office, the INS came up with a rather distressing response. It is not uncommon for visitors from Taiwan—many of whom may need assistance with an English language form—to enter simply "China" as their country of citizenship and country of residence. (Incidentally, the Form I-94 encourages such an abridgment by allowing only 15 block letters for these entries—not quite enough to print "Republic of China.") By way of verification, the number of F-1 visas issued to students from Taiwan is much lower than it should be. The discrepancy is not nearly as great for the J-1 visas (albeit in the same direction) not only because official visitors would be much more careful in identifying their country of citizenship and residence but also because the number of J-1 visas issued to residents of Taiwan is much smaller.

To complete the INS story, it should be noted that even if the forms were filled out properly, the INS would not be able to provide the number of Chinese students in the country in any one year. Such an estimate would require not only statistics on the number of arrivals, but also on the number who returned to China. But with departure controls much more lax, it is virtually impossible for INS to estimate the number of annual departures or the number

---

[5] *1985 Statistical Yearbook of the Immigration and Naturalization Service* (Washington, D.C.: U.S. Department of Justice, 1986), pp. 113 and 120.

who have overstayed their visas. For a clearer understanding of the problem we must return to the two-part I-94 form. The top part, the "arrival record," is relinquished to INS on entry; the bottom part, the "departure record," is retained by the individual until departure, when it must be "reunited" with the arrival record. However, this does not always happen. All too often the departure forms are not returned—curiously the responsibility of the carrier—or not turned in to the appropriate INS office; and even when they are properly collected and turned in to INS, the prescribed process of matching the departure and arrival sections of the I-94 forms is of low priority. As a result, students of all nationalities tend to overstay their visas, and so long as they do not break any laws, no one is likely to search them out. What this means, of course, is that even if specifically tasked, the INS could not readily produce internally reliable data from which a figure for the number of Chinese currently in the United States could be derived. And, of course, the grapevine works; it does not take long for arriving foreign students to discover the impotence of American immigration laws.

To end on a more positive note, the INS has become keenly aware of the special and varied problems associated with the heavy flow of Chinese students and scholars to this country, and the corrective measures now being taken should eventually improve statistics on visitors from China.

STATISTICS FROM VISA APPLICATIONS AND USIA DATA TAPES

Now let us consider the data from visa applications and the USIA's IAP-66 forms—the two sources of the statistics used in this study.

Visa applications submitted to the U.S. Embassy and the four Consulates in China constitute the most accurate and useful statistics on Chinese students and scholars in the United States. To review the process, a Chinese scholar or student wishing to come to the United States must first get approval from the work unit. The written approval is used to obtain a Chinese passport, which must be presented at the U.S. Embassy or Consulates when application is made for a nonimmigrant visa. The F-1 visas are generally issued to students who develop their own program of study and get financial assistance for travel and tuition from relatives or friends. Most of the J-1 visas are issued to scholars (many of international standing), selected and supported by the Chinese government or one of its subordinate entities, and are therefore considered to be "officially sponsored," even when not funded by Beijing. All visa applications contain considerable detail about the intended program of study in the United States, as well as personal characteristics of the applicants. One reason for so much detail is to prove to the consular officer that the applicant has sufficient ties to China (professional and/or family) to assure his or her return and therefore increase his or her eligibility for a nonimmigrant visa.

There is no reason to doubt the accuracy of the number of visas issued by the U.S. Embassy and Consulates in China and, while some of the responses on the applications may be subject to "adjustments" that a prospective student might deem necessary or desirable, the completed forms are rich in information not otherwise obtainable. The problem is that while we have accurate totals of the number of visas issued, the Department of State does not keep track of the returnees (an INS task), making it impossible to estimate the actual number of Chinese students and scholars in the United States. Moreover, neither the Department of State's Visa Office in Washington, nor any other government office has the responsibility or the wherewithal to analyze the information available in the visa applications. In other words, this rich source of information went untapped prior to CSCPRC's first effort to process and analyze these data.[6]

The second source of statistical data for J-1 scholars and students is the IAP-66 form issued by the USIA. Using information obtained from the student's application form, universities or other institutions in the United States fill out Form IAP-66 to document the applicant's qualifications under one of the programs designated by the USIA. They also show the amount and source of financial support and are submitted with the student's passport to the U.S. visa offices at the embassy or consulates. Form IAP-66 is also filled out by any exchange visitor requesting an extension of the ongoing program, wishing to transfer to a different program, or requesting a permit to allow a visit by a member of his or her immediate family.

---

[6]David M. Lampton et al., *A Relationship Restored: Trends in U.S.-China Educational Exchanges, 1978-1984* (Washington, D.C.: National Academy Press, 1986).

As shown in the next chapter, the statistics on those entering new programs and those extending their stay is of considerable value in estimating the net number of students and scholars in this country. Since F-1 students are privately sponsored, they do not have to fill out Form IAP-66, although they must present an affidavit of financial support to assure the authorities that they will not become public charges or be forced to work.

5
Statistics on Trends and Characteristics of Exchange Participants from China

We are now ready to turn to the statistics themselves. Although supplemented with more recent figures and some previously unavailable data, the basic trends and conclusions are, for the most part, identical to those described by David Lampton in the earlier study.[1] The commentary that follows is essentially a "walk through the data" with a minimum of "table climbing." It should also be noted that some of the issues inherent in the statistics were discussed more fully or from a somewhat different perspective in the first part of this study.

There are several ways in which the statistics could have been organized and discussed. In attempting to take into consideration the special interests of the various constituencies, the analysis was divided into the following three parts: (1) "students and scholars," which makes possible some general conclusions about everyone involved in the exchange programs; (2) "students," which allows comparisons between the J-1 and F-1 visa holders in this category; and (3) "research scholars," which focuses on the more senior segment of the participants.

---

[1]David M. Lampton et al., *A Relationship Restored: Trends in U.S.-China Educational Exchanges, 1978-1984* (Washington, D.C.: National Academy Press, 1986).

J-1 AND F-1 STUDENTS AND SCHOLARS

The visas issued by the U.S. Embassy and Consulates in China—and it is rare for an issued visa to go unused—provide us with the most reliable information on the number of students and scholars entering the United States. Table 5-1 presents the number of J-1 and F-1 visas issued between 1979 and 1986. The figures show an annual increase in the number of J-1 visas, but a considerable fluctuation in the case of F-1 visas, which were subject to more policy shifts. For the period under discussion, only in 1980 were there more F-1 than J-1 visas issued, reflecting a rapid surge in applications by privately sponsored students in the immediate postnormalization period, while it took more time (and red tape) to start up the flow of government-sponsored scholars. For the other seven years, the proportion of F-1 visas ranged from a low of 23.2 percent of the total in 1983 to 43.3 percent in 1981.

With the opening up of additional U.S. Consulates in China, it is interesting to consider the trends of visas issued by the Consulates and the Embassy in Beijing (see Tables 5-2 and 5-3). As might be expected, the Embassy has been issuing by far the largest proportion

TABLE 5-1 Number of Visas Issued to PRC Students and Scholars, 1979-1987

Year	J-1 Visas	F-1 Visas	Total
1979	807	523	1,330
1980	1,986	2,338	4,324
1981	3,066	2,341	5,407
1982	3,327	1,153	4,480
1983	3,328	1,003	4,331
1984	4,420	1,677	6,097
1985	6,912	3,001	9,913
1986	7,673	5,038	12,711
1987 (fiscal)	8,179	5,235	13,414
Total	39,698	22,309	62,007

NOTE: The use of fiscal year for 1987 excludes the last three months of 1987, but double counts the same three months for 1986. The net effect on the total is insignificant.

SOURCE: 1979-1986: Consular reports, U.S. Department of State. 1987: Visa Office, U.S. Department of State, Washington, D.C.

TABLE 5-2 Number of J-1 Visas Issued by Each U.S. Embassy and
Consulate in China, 1979-1986

Year	Total	Beijing	Shanghai	Guangzhou	Shenyang	Chengdu
1979	807	807	--	--	--	--
1980	1,986	1,930	45	11	--	--
1981	3,066	2,631	366	69	--	--
1982	3,327	2,404	734	189	--	--
1983	3,328	2,297	812	219	--	--
1984	4,420	3,177	1,011	213	19	--
1985	6,912	4,315	1,809	515	266	7
1986	7,673	4,261	2,079	565	402	366

NOTE: Figures begin with opening of Embassies and Consulates.

SOURCE: Record of issued visas.

TABLE 5-3 Number of F-1 Visas Issued by Each U.S. Embassy and Consulate
in China, 1979-1986

Year	Total	Beijing	Shanghai	Guangzhou	Shenyang	Chengdu
1979	523	523	--	--	--	--
1980	2,338	994	679	665	--	--
1981	2,341	721	1,079	541	--	--
1982	1,153	319	551	283	--	--
1983	1,003	383	419	201	--	--
1984	1,677	704	642	304	27	--
1985	3,001	1,405	1,002	461	126	7
1986	5,038	1,942	2,019	821	206	50

NOTE: Figures begin with opening of Embassies and Consulates.

SOURCE: Record of issued visas.

of J-1 visas, while most of the F-1 visas were issued by the Consulates. With the exception of a very small decline in 1984 in Guangzhou, all Consulates showed a steady increase in the number of J-1 visas issued. In the case of F-1 visas, the fluctuations were much more evident. As local areas are encouraged to arrange for their own J-1 students and scholars, the number of visas issued by the Consulates should continue to increase, with the new Consulates in Shenyang and Chengdu showing the most rapid growth. Unless China introduces restrictions on F-1 visas, these too should show a more rapid increase outside of Beijing. In other words, whether the total number of visas issued in China increases or decreases, the proportion issued by the Embassy would probably decline.

An examination of the changes that have occurred in the financial support for J-1 students and scholars over the years is extremely revealing (see Tables 5-4 and 5-5). As the number of students and scholars increased, so naturally did the funding, with some half a billion U.S. dollars being spent from all sources in the course of the seven years under review. More striking, however, is the extent of the internal changes in the funding. While in absolute numbers the amount of funding from the Chinese government increased almost every year, there has been a drastic decrease in the share it provides (down from 54 percent in 1979 to 17 percent in 1985) and a corresponding increase in the support provided by American universities (up from 18 to 57 percent). The funding shift is even more dramatic for continuing students and scholars—in 1985 the Chinese government contributed only 12 percent of their funding.[2] Once in this country, and encouraged by their government, Chinese scholars and students quickly become adept at finding sources of funds from U.S. universities and other institutions. To some extent their success in this regard demonstrates an ability to compete against both domestic and other foreign students, but they also have an advantage not available to others. Although small in percentage terms, large amounts of money have been spent by U.S. foundations (Asia Foundation, Ford Foundation, Luce Foundation, and others) to support Chinese students and scholars. In other words, for the Chinese the competition for academic funds is not a zero-sum game; more than likely the money allocated to support the Chinese would not have been spent on students from any other country. Of course, it should be kept in mind that most foreign students cannot rely on their governments for support and must use their own funds or seek subsidies from U.S. universities, so that the Chinese experience is simply approaching the norm.

Available data also permits us to approximate expenditures from

---

[2]A Chinese report that from 1979 through 1984 Beijing spent US$116 million to send students abroad to *all* countries (*CD*, Nov. 30, 1984, p. 1) seems somewhat low when compared with the US$97 million spent in the United States for the same years, as shown in Table 5-4. The difference may be explained, in part, by the higher tuition costs in the United States, definitional differences, and conversion factors from yuan to dollars.

TABLE 5-4 Financial Support by Source for PRC J-1 Students and Scholars, 1979-1985
(US$ in thousands)

Source of Funds	1979	1980	1981	1982	1983	1984	1985	Total
PRC government	3,968	7,729	15,011	17,006	25,967	27,623	22,280	119,584
Personal funds	187	789	1,982	2,547	5,353	8,832	12,013	31,703
U.S. government	550	1,490	2,586	3,298	4,499	5,000	5,295	22,718
U.S. university	1,354	6,487	17,117	24,988	38,584	53,621	76,423	218,574
U.S. foundation	263	814	1,003	1,113	1,800	2,314	3,151	10,458
U.S. corporation	17	32	557	602	506	343	758	2,815
International organization	70	203	606	636	1,233	1,161	1,140	5,049
Other	983	1,725	2,951	4,582	6,285	9,436	12,220	38,182
Total	7,392	19,269	41,813	54,772	84,227	108,330	133,280	449,083
Number of students and scholars for whom data on finances were available	808	2,235	4,520	5,802	8,228	9,876	11,185	
Percentage of total	79	82	81	83	84	86	87	

NOTE: Dollar amounts were raised proportionately to adjust for the 15 to 20 percent for whom financial data were not available. Comparable information is not available for those on F-1 visas.

SOURCE: USIA data tapes.

TABLE 5-5 Percentage Distribution of Sources of Financial Support for PRC J-1 Students and Scholars in All Categories, 1979-1985

Source of Funds	1979	1980	1981	1982	1983	1984	1985
PRC government	54	40	36	31	31	25	17
Personal funds	3	4	5	5	6	8	9
U.S. government	7	8	6	6	5	5	4
U.S. university	18	34	41	46	46	49	57
U.S. foundation	4	4	2	2	2	2	2
U.S. corporation	--	--	1	1	1	--	1
International organization	1	1	1	1	1	1	1
Other	13	9	7	8	7	9	9
Total	100	100	100	100	100	100	100

NOTE: The symbol "--" indicates a value less than 0.5 percent.

SOURCE: USIA data tapes.

TABLE 5-6 Average Annual Expenditure per PRC J-1 Student or Scholar

Year	Number in U.S. with J-1 Visas	Amount Spent (US$ thousands)	Dollars per Student or Scholar
1979	1,025	7,392	7,200
1980	2,720	19,269	7,100
1981	5,568	41,813	7,500
1982	6,985	54,772	7,800
1983	9,779	84,227	8,600
1984	11,505	108,330	9,400
1985	12,899	133,280	10,300

SOURCE: First column, from Table 5-27; Second column, from Table 5-4.

all sources per J-1 student and scholar (see Table 5-6). The reasonableness and consistency of the resulting figures can be seen as providing an independent validation for the calculated number of J-1 students in the United States.

There are no surprises in the geographic distribution of the students and scholars who come to the United States (see Table 5-7). In 1985 34 percent of the J-1 visa holders were from Beijing and 15 percent from Shanghai; of the F-1 visa holders, again 34 percent were from Beijing but a much larger proportion, 26 percent, were from Shanghai and 13 percent were from Guangdong Province, primarily from its capital, Guangzhou. The reason for F-1 students going abroad in large numbers from the coastal provinces of south and central China is found in recent history. The large number of immigrants from these regions in the last part of the nineteenth and the first half of the twentieth centuries now provide succeeding generations with many well-to-do relatives in the United States willing to support their education. With incomes on the rise, there are now families in China itself (especially in the large port cities) who have accumulated adequate savings to send an offspring abroad. For privately sponsored students, the location of the U.S Embassy or Consulates in their city would also greatly facilitate the visa-filing process. In general, it is safe to say that the overwhelming proportion of all students and scholars coming to this country (and going to other countries as well) is from the large urban municipalities, which have not only the better key universities, but also a better-educated adult (parental) populace.

Although still prominent, the bunching phenomenon is not quite as great when we look at the geographic areas of scholars and students by place of birth rather than place of residence. The reason, of course, is that the magnet of Beijing, Shanghai, Guangzhou, and other large municipalities has been functioning for decades, first drawing the parents, but even if not the parents, then their most-talented offspring through the college-entrance examinations.

What this means is that foreign education will only accentuate the already existing concentration of the highly trained manpower (along with other economic and capital resources) in the large metropolitan areas of China's eastern provinces. Because of deficiencies in the primary and secondary school systems, young people from the interior still find it difficult to compete for the limited slots available in domestic four-year universities—especially the more prominent key institutions—and rural youth find it to be an almost insurmountable hurdle. At this stage in China's development, however, and juxtaposing her goals and priorities with the shortage of trained professionals, Beijing cannot yet afford the "luxury" of giving much more than lip service to educational egalitarianism.

TABLE 5-7 Percentage Distribution of PRC Students and Scholars by Place of Residence in China, 1983-1985

Place of Residence in China	1983		1984		1985	
	F-1 Visas	J-1 Visas	F-1 Visas	J-1 Visas	F-1 Visas	J-1 Visas
Beijing	25	37	26	32	34	34
Guangdong	17	5	15	4	13	6
Hube	2	5	2	5	2	4
Jiangsu	4	5	3	7	3	5
Shanghai	33	14	32	17	26	15
Sichuan	1	5	--	4		4
All other provinces	18	29	20	31	21	32
Total	100	100	100	100	100	100
(N)	(947)	(3,150)	(1,491)	(3,330)	(2,679)	(6,026)

NOTE: The symbol "--" indicates a value less than 0.5 percent. Percentage of missing data excluded from totals is 2 percent or less for all years.

SOURCE: Records of issued visas.

J-1 AND F-1 STUDENTS

Table 5-8 clearly shows the very different trends between students with J-1 and F-1 visas. While it took several years to mount the official exchange of students (most of the early arrivals being scholars), once the opportunity became available, thousands of young people quickly found the way and the means to get into U.S. universities on their own. The extremely large number of F-1 visas issued since 1985 is somewhat surprising in view of Beijing's stated desire to eliminate most of the privately sponsored graduate education abroad.

Financial support sources for the J-1 students, as derived from USIA data tapes, were discussed above, but there is also some financial assistance information available from the visa data, which permits some comparisons between the J-1 and F-1 students (see Table 5-9). The figures in the table require no explanation, with the exception of the extremely high increase in 1985 in the "other or a combination of sources" category. The high proportion in this category is due to the practice of combining the funding from several sources—reflecting experience that took several years to acquire.

TABLE 5-8 Number of Visas Issued to PRC Students, 1979-1986

| Year | J-1 Visas | | F-1 Visas | | |
	No.	%	No.	%	Total
1979	145	22	523	78	668
1980	336	13	2,338	87	2,674
1981	680	23	2,341	77	3,021
1982	950	45	1,153	55	2,103
1983	1,572	61	1,003	39	2,575
1984	1,783	52	1,677	48	3,460
1985	2,507	46	3,001	54	5,508
1986	(3,069)	38	5,038	62	(8,107)
1987 (fiscal)	(3,272)	38	5,235	62	(8,507)
Total	14,314	39	22,309	61	36,623

NOTE: The use of fiscal year for 1987 excludes the last three months of 1987, but double counts the same three months for 1986. The net effect on the total is insignificant.

SOURCES: F-1 visas from consular reports, U.S. Department of State. J-1 visas, 1979-1985, from USIA data tapes; 1986 and 1987, estimates made by distributing reported totals by applying the average ratio of student J-1s to total J-1s for the preceding three years.

For the J-1s the most common combination is U.S. university and Chinese government; for the F-1s it is U.S. university with Chinese family, Chinese work unit, and U.S. relative, in that order.

Tables 5-10, 5-11, and 5-12 show some significant differences and trends in the personal characteristics of both officially and privately sponsored students.

During the early years of the post-Mao exchanges, China had few young, capable students to send abroad, but there were older, more experienced scholars (many of them trained earlier overseas) looking for opportunities to spend a year or two abroad to catch up with developments that had taken place in their fields during the isolation years of the Cultural Revolution. Now the average age for the holders of J-1 visas is significantly lower, with about two-thirds

TABLE 5-9 Percentage Distribution of PRC J-1 and F-1 Students by Stated Source of Financial Support, 1983-1985

| | Year Visa Issued | | | | | |
| | 1983 | | 1984 | | 1985 | |
Stated Source of Financial Support	F-1 Visas	J-1 Visas	F-1 Visas	J-1 Visas	F-1 Visas	J-1 Visas
Self, savings, or family in China	--	--	2	1	1	1
Chinese government or work unit	1	46	2	19	4	22
U.S. relatives or private individual	76	4	74	9	43	3
U.S. government	0	1	0	1	0	--
U.S. university	12	36	16	57	19	42
U.S. foundation/ philanthropy	0	4	--	2	--	1
International organization	0	5	--	2	--	1
Other or combination of sources	11	5	5	8	33	30
Total	100	100	100	100	100	100
(N)	(942)	(2,131)	(1,502)	(1,145)	(2,388)	(2,436)

NOTE: Number of individuals missing from totals is less than 5 percent, except for F-1 students in 1985, who account for 12 percent. The symbol "--" indicates a value less than 0.5 percent.

SOURCE: Records of issued visas.

falling into the 20–29 age group; and, since many have also spent a year or two working, they most likely fall in the upper half of that age cohort (Table 5-10). One might well have expected students holding F-1 visas to be younger, but in fact for two of the three years for which data are available, the reverse was true.

Between 1980 and 1985 about one-fifth of the government-sponsored students were women (Table 5-11)—only slightly lower than the proportion of women in Chinese institutions of higher education. Predictably, the discrepancy in the male–female ratio among students with F-1 visas is not nearly as great. When it comes to fields of study, there is a significant difference between men and women students with J-1 visas. Whereas most of the men are enrolled in engineering and the physical sciences, the largest proportion of women choose American studies, library and archival science, and health sciences, in that order.[3]

While there is no significant difference in the ages of the J-1 and F-1 students and scholars, there is a large discrepancy in the marital status of the two groups (Table 5-12). Marriage and family ties are presumably paramount considerations in making the decision to return or remain in the United States, so that it is probably easier for married individuals to receive approval for foreign study; thus the large proportion of married J-1s. On the other hand, it is safe to assume that the overwhelming proportion of F-1 females are both young and single.

Since the presence of a spouse undoubtedly influences the return decision, it is surprising to see an extremely large increase in J-2 and F-2 visas, which are issued to family members (mostly spouses) of Chinese students. Prior to 1984, the number of these visas issued each year was below 100 for both categories. In 1984, however, 318 J-2 and 94 F-2 visas were issued; in 1985, 2,030 J-2s and 244 F-2s; and in 1986, 2,022 J-2s and 559 F-2s. These increases occurred despite some clear statements by Chinese officials that the issuance of permits for spouses to apply for visas to join their student mates would be drastically restricted. Moreover, once they arrive in the United States, many of the spouses become students in their own right.

---

[3]Lampton, *A Relationship Restored*, p. 188. Although data are for the 1979–1984 period, there is no reason to expect any major changes since then.

TABLE 5-10 Percentage Distribution of PRC J-1 and F-1 Students Entering a New Program by Age, 1979-1985

	Year Program Began									
Age	1979 J-1	1980 J-1	1981 J-1	1982 J-1	1983 J-1	1983 F-1	1984 J-1	1984 F-1	1985 J-1	1985 F-1
Under 20 years	0	--	1	1	1	5	1	3	1	3
20 to 29 years	21	20	30	54	66	58	62	60	63	63
30 to 39 years	64	49	40	31	24	33	26	32	27	31
40 to 49 years	14	25	23	9	7	3	8	4	6	3
50 to 59 years	1	4	2	2	1	--	1	--	1	--
60 years and older	0	2	5	2	1	--	1	--	1	--
Total	100	100	100	100	100	100	100	100	100	100
(N)	(145)	(366)	(680)	(950)	(1,572)	(949)	(1,783)	(1,517)	(2,507)	(2,727)

NOTE: Age distribution for F-1 visa holders not available prior to 1983. The symbol "--" indicates a value less than 0.5 percent.

SOURCE: Figures for J-1 students are from USIA data tapes. Figures for F-1 students are from records of issued visas.

TABLE 5-11 Percentage of Women Among Students and
Scholars, 1979-1985

Year	J-1 Scholars	J-1 Students	F-1 Students
1979	14	13	n.a.
1980	16	18	n.a.
1981	15	18	n.a.
1982	17	18	n.a.
1983	18	17	37
1984	20	19	45
1985	24	20	41

SOURCE: J-1 figures for those entering a new program
are from USIA data tapes; F-1 figures are from records
of issued visas.

TABLE 5-12 Percentage Distribution by Marital Status of PRC J-1 and F-1
Students, 1983-1985

| Marital Status | Year Visa Issued | | | | | |
| | 1983 | | 1984 | | 1985 | |
	J-1	F-1	J-1	F-1	J-1	F-1
Single	37	69	38	66	46	65
Married	62	30	61	33	54	34
Previously married	--	1	1	--	--	1
Total	100	100	100	100	100	100
(N)	(2,190)	(949)	(1,196)	(1,514)	(2,519)	(2,721)

NOTE: The symbol "--" indicates a value less than 0.5 percent.

SOURCE: Records of issued visas.

The data in Tables 5-13 and 5-14 are not comparable (occupation
for J-1s and educational background for F-1s), but they do contain
some interesting information about the backgrounds of the students
in the two groups. As might be expected, professionally, the stand-
ings of J-1 visa holders are much higher, with about three-quarters
coming from the ranks of university teachers or professors and of

TABLE 5-13 Percentage Distribution by Occupation in China of PRC J-1 Students Entering New Programs, 1979-1985

Occupation	Year Program Began						
	1979	1980	1981	1982	1983	1984	1985
Government	15	8	6	6	2	4	4
University teaching	20	31	27	28	28	30	37
University graduate student	37	39	45	42	48	44	39
University under- graduate student	12	6	11	18	16	13	10
Secondary or ele- mentary school teachers	3	3	2	1	1	1	1
Business	1	1	2	1	1	1	2
Other organizations	12	13	7	4	4	5	5
Total	100	100	100	100	100	100	100
(N)	(145)	(366)	(680)	(950)	(1,572)	(1,783)	(2,507)

SOURCE: USIA data tapes.

TABLE 5-14 Percentage Distribution by Educational Background of PRC F-1 Students, 1983-1985

Highest Level of Education Completed	Year Visa Issued		
	1983	1984	1985
Middle school or less	15	11	6
Technical school	14	4	8
College/university, no degree	13	6	8
College/university, degree	56	75	64
Graduate study	3	4	14
Total	100	100	100
(N)	(850)	(1,229)	(1,667)

NOTE: Distributions are based on incomplete totals: missing 11 percent in 1983, 19 percent in 1984, and 39 percent in 1985.

SOURCE: Records of issued visas.

TABLE 5-15 Percentage Distribution by Field of Study of PRC J-1 Students
Entering New Programs, 1979-1985

Field of Study	Year Program Began						
	1979	1980	1981	1982	1983	1984	1985
Agriculture	0	1	1	2	3	4	4
American studies	1	0	--	--	1	1	--
Architecture	1	0	--	--	1	--	--
Business management	2	2	1	3	2	3	3
Computer science	9	4	3	3	4	4	3
Education	3	4	5	4	4	3	3
Engineering	34	24	14	17	23	22	20
English as a second language (ESL)	1	5	3	1	1	1	2
Health sciences	4	3	3	3	2	3	3
Humanities	3	6	7	6	3	5	6
Law	1	2	1	1	1	1	2
Library and archival science	0	1	--	--	1	1	1
Life sciences	7	6	5	9	10	8	9
Mathematics	4	4	7	7	6	7	9
Physical sciences	21	26	37	33	29	26	25
Social sciences	8	7	5	7	7	7	9
Other or not stated	2	5	7	3	3	4	3
Total	100	100	100	100	100	100	100
(N)	(145)	(366)	(680)	(950)	(1,572)	(1,783)	(2,507)

NOTE: The symbol "--" indicates a value less than 0.5 percent.

SOURCE: USIA data tapes.

graduate students (see Table 5-13). Most of the F-1 students also
have college degrees and an increasing proportion have done graduate
work, but some of these privately sponsored individuals have not gone
beyond middle or technical schools (see Table 5-14).

Among the more interesting and important information con-
tained in the visa records and the USIA tapes is the distribution
of students by field of study (see Tables 5-15 and 5-16). Here, too,
there are no surprises. Since science and technology are the priority
fields identified by the Four Modernizations policy, the proportion of
J-1 visa holders in engineering and the physical sciences has hovered
at about 50 percent throughout the period under consideration. On
the other hand, the F-1s, who are freer to choose their own majors,
have been selecting a much broader range of specializations, with en-

gineering, humanities, physical sciences, business management, and computer sciences leading the way, in that order.

The Chinese Embassy in Washington has also compiled statistics on all J-1 students and scholars by fields of study, but with a much finer breakdown. If combined into the broader categories shown in Table 5-15, the percentages derived from the Chinese figures seem to correspond fairly closely to ours. The PRC Embassy figures shown in Table 5-17 are for the latter part of 1986 and include all major fields with more than 100 scholars and students. The detailed breakdown shows some interesting relationships between fields and between scholars and graduate students within fields. What is per-

TABLE 5-16 Percentage Distribution by Intended Field of Study of PRC F-1 Students, 1983-1985

Intended	Year Visa Issued		
Field of Study	1983	1984	1985
Agriculture	1	--	1
American studies	--	1	--
Architecture	1	--	1
Business management	9	8	11
Computer science	13	12	10
Education	3	5	5
Engineering	23	17	17
English as a second language (ESL)	1	0	0
Health sciences	4	3	4
Humanities	15	16	15
Law	--	--	--
Library and archival science	--	--	--
Life sciences	5	6	6
Mathematics	5	4	5
Physical sciences	14	11	14
Social sciences	4	5	6
Other	2	10	3
Total	100	100	100
(N)	(911)[a]	(1,232)[b]	(2,218)[b]

NOTE: The symbol "--" indicates a value less than 0.5 percent.
[a] Missing data excluded from total, 4 percent.
[b] Missing data excluded from total, 19 percent.

SOURCE: Records of issued visas.

TABLE 5-17　Major Fields with More Than 100 Students and Scholars

Major	Total	Scholars	Graduate Students	Under- graduates	% of Total
Physics	1,408	391	1,000	17	13.01
Chemistry	1,017	392	617	8	9.40
Medicine	724	622	97	5	6.69
Computer science	711	368	341	2	6.57
Electrical engineering	647	324	322	1	5.98
Mathematics	536	97	434	5	4.95
Mechanical engineering	507	268	237	2	4.69
Language	468	318	135	15	4.33
Biochemistry	422	155	264	3	3.90
Biology	333	150	181	2	3.08
Economics	227	66	152	9	2.10
Civil engineering	223	108	113	2	2.06
Material engineering	223	120	102	1	2.06
"Undecided"	195	99	91	5	1.80
Law	154	78	68	8	1.42
Management	149	93	53	3	1.38
Chemical engineering	129	70	59	0	1.19
Education	129	63	62	4	1.19
Business administration	126	74	50	2	1.16
Literature	117	64	52	1	1.08
Molecular biology	114	60	54	0	1.05
Geology	112	35	76	1	1.04
Other	2,148	972	1,156	20	19.87
Total	10,819	4,987	5,716	116	100.00
(%)		(46.1)	(52.8)	(1.1)	

SOURCE: Preliminary figures provided by the PRC Embassy, Washington, D.C.

haps most striking about the figures is that over 20 percent of the students and scholars are in physics and chemistry; if only graduate students are considered, almost 20 percent are in physics alone. As discussed in the first part of this report, it is just this overemphasis on the physical sciences that is, at least in part, responsible for the complaints of returnees about facilities, equipment, and the inability to do research of their own choosing. And it is also this skewed distribution of specializations that has led to recent policies designed to encourage individuals going abroad to subordinate their own interests to the more practical and immediate needs of the country.

Table 5-18 shows the rapid acceleration in the number of doctorates earned by Chinese citizens in the various fields of science and engineering between 1980 and 1986—almost two-thirds in the sciences. Considering the number of Chinese students already enrolled in PhD programs, the annual number of degrees that they earn should continue to increase for a number of years.

In connection with the distribution of students by field at all academic levels, it is interesting to note one striking (but not surprising) similarity between domestic college students and those going abroad. In both instances they tend to avoid majors that will take them out of the cities and into less hospitable environments. Thus, even though

TABLE 5-18 PRC Citizens Awarded Science and Engineering Doctorates by Major Field

Major Field	Year of Doctorate							Total 1980-86
	1980	1981	1982	1983	1984	1985	1986	
Total, science and engineering	1	-	2	8	39	90	137	277
Total, sciences	-	-	1	5	23	60	95	184
Physical sciences	-	-	1	1	10	25	52	89
Physics and astronomy	-	-	-	-	7	19	42	68
Chemistry	-	-	1	1	3	6	10	21
Earth, atmospheric and marine sciences	-	-	-	1	3	6	7	17
Life sciences	-	-	-	1	2	10	8	21
Agricultural sciences	-	-	-	-	-	1	1	2
Biological sciences	-	-	-	1	2	9	7	19
Mathematics	-	-	-	2	7	13	20	42
Computer/information sciences	-	-	-	-	-	5	6	11
Social sciences	-	-	-	-	1	1	2	4
Total, engineering	1	-	1	3	16	30	42	93
Chemical	-	-	-	-	-	3	2	5
Civil	-	-	-	-	-	2	2	4
Electrical	-	-	-	1	5	7	11	25
Mechanical	-	-	-	2	1	10	10	23
Material science	-	-	-	-	5	2	3	10
Total, nonscience and engineering	-	2	-	1	1	-	2	6
Total, all fields	1	2	2	9	40	90	139	285

NOTE: There are some discrepancies between the annual figures and the totals reported in the source. Of the 152,488 doctorates awarded in S&E by U.S. universities between 1970 and 1979, 36,925 (24 percent) went to non-U.S. citizens; of the 96,954 such degrees awarded between 1980 and 1986, 29,734 (31 percent) went to non-U.S. citizens.

SOURCE: Statistics compiled from Science and Engineering Doctorates: 1960-86 (Washington, D.C.: National Science Foundation, 1988). NSF 88-309, pp. 140-150.

TABLE 5-19 Most Common States of Residence in the United States for PRC J-1 Students, 1983-1985 (percent)

State of Residence While Studying in U.S.	Year Visa Issued		
	1983	1984	1985
New York	14	13	13
California	12	10	9
Massachusetts	6	6	7
Pennsylvania	6	7	6
Illinois	5	5	6
Ohio	4	6	5
Indiana	4	4	5
Michigan	6	4	5
Texas	4	4	5
New Jersey	2	3	3
All other states	37	38	36
Total	100	100	100
(N)	(2,190)	(1,199)	(2,524)

SOURCE: Records of issued visas.

the demand for college slots is much greater than their supply, Chinese planners and university administrators complain that "departments of hydrology, agriculture, geology, mining, and petroleum and mineral exploration still find it difficult to enroll enough students."[4] Avoidance of these majors is just as evident among students going abroad.

California and New York have by far the largest proportions of both J-1 and F-1 students (Tables 5-19 and 5-20), although they generally attend different types of colleges and universities. With cost undoubtedly a serious consideration, most students choose public rather than private universities (Tables 5-21 and 5-22), Columbia University being the only private institution with large numbers of both J-1 and F-1 students.

[4]Li Xing, "Who Will Go to College?" *CD*, Aug. 21, 1987, p. 5.

TABLE 5-20 Most Common States of Residence in the United States for PRC F-1 Students, 1983-1985 (percent)

State of Residence While Studying in U.S.	Year Visa Issued		
	1983	1984	1985
California	24	20	20
New York	18	20	17
Texas	5	6	5
Illinois	6	5	5
Massachusetts	5	4	4
Pennsylvania	2	4	4
Ohio	3	3	4
Michigan	3	3	3
Washington	2	3	2
New Jersey	3	3	2
Utah	2	3	2
All other states	27	26	33
Total	100	100	100
(N)	(938)	(1,517)	(2,727)

SOURCE: Records of issued visas.

TABLE 5-21 U.S. Colleges and Universities with the Largest Number of PRC J-1 Students Enrolling, 1983-1985

College or University	Number
University of Michigan	152
Purdue University	117
University of Pittsburgh	111
Columbia University	109
University of Minnesota	108
University of Illinois, Champaign-Urbana	104
Cornell University	101
University of California, Los Angeles	93
Ohio State University	93
Stanford University	86

SOURCE: Records of issued visas. Figures do not necessarily reflect actual enrollment.

TABLE 5-22 U.S. Colleges and Universities with the
Largest Number of PRC F-1 Students Enrolling, 1983-1985

College or University	Number
City University of New York, City College	117
City University of New York, Queens College	91
Hunter College	90
Columbia University	88
University of California, Los Angeles	74
San Francisco State University	67
University of Maryland, College Park	60
University of Houston	57
LaGuardia Community College	57
The Loop College (two-year)	56

SOURCE: Records of issued visas. Figures do not
necessarily reflect actual enrollment.

J-1 VISITING SCHOLARS

Visiting scholars make up the largest percentage of Chinese exchange visitors with J-1 visas. They do not come to the United States to enroll in specific degree programs, but rather to conduct research and study on their own. In general, they must have an established reputation in China or a relatively long and successful academic career or research experience when selected for the program. Because of these prerequisites, the characteristics of visiting scholars are quite different from students with J-1 visas.

With established reputations, J-1 visiting scholars tend to be much older than the students; until 1983 there were few under the age of 30 (Table 5-23). This is changing, however, and in 1985, 11 percent were 20 to 29 years of age. While most still fall in the 40 to 49 years of age cohort, between 1979 and 1985 the percentage in this category steadily decreased and the percentage of scholars between 30 and 39 years of age has steadily increased. In fact, the new regulations state specifically that 50 should be the age limit for advanced studies personnel and visiting scholars, with some possible exceptions for full professors going abroad for short periods. Although the percentage of female scholars has been increasing since 1979, it is still low, closely paralleling both the proportion and the increase

TABLE 5-23 Percentage Distribution of PRC J-1 Research Scholars Entering a
New Program, by Age, 1979-1985

Age	Year Program Began						
	1979	1980	1981	1982	1983	1984	1985
Under 20 years	1	--	--	--	--	0	0
20 to 29 years	1	1	1	2	3	6	11
30 to 39 years	25	15	14	15	18	21	23
40 to 49 years	66	65	65	60	54	47	44
50 to 59 years	6	13	12	17	18	19	17
60 years and older	1	4	8	6	6	8	6
Total	100	100	100	100	100	100	100
(N)	(631)	(1,232)	(2,036)	(1,694)	(1,861)	(2,188)	(3,049)

NOTE: The symbol "--" indicates a value less than 0.5 percent.

SOURCE: USIA data tapes.

TABLE 5-24 Percentage Distribution of PRC J-1 Research Scholars Entering a New Program,
by Occupation in China, 1979-1985

Occupation	Year Program Began						
	1979	1980	1981	1982	1983	1984	1985
Government	12	8	7	10	12	11	8
University teaching or research	69	75	74	71	71	69	73
University graduate student	2	1	1	1	1	1	3
Business	--	1	1	2	2	2	2
Other organizations	17	14	16	15	13	16	13
Total	100	100	100	100	100	100	100
(N)	(631)	(1,232)	(2,036)	(1,694)	(1,861)	(2,188)	(3,049)

NOTE: The symbol "--" indicates a value less than 0.5 percent.

SOURCE: USIA data tapes.

for female students with J-1 visas (see Table 5-11). In terms of their
background, the vast majority of visiting scholars have been teaching
at universities, although a significant percentage have been from
government institutions, which would include the various academies
of sciences and research institutes under the production ministries
(Table 5-24).

The J-1 research scholars are selected, approved, and, one can say, employed by the Chinese government, but who pays for their studies in the United States? As in the case of J-1 students, in 1985 almost half of the funding came from U.S. universities, with only 23 percent supported by the PRC (Table 5-25). As in the case of students, since 1979 there has been a decreasing trend in the *proportion* of funding by the Chinese government and a corresponding increase in support by American universities. Taken together, the two sources accounted for 71 percent of the funding for J-1 scholars in 1985, a decrease from 83 percent in 1979.

Chinese visiting scholars who come to the United States tend to represent a much narrower range of specializations (Table 5-26) than do the students. Over the years about three-quarters of the scholars have been doing work in engineering, physical sciences, health sciences, and life sciences, with small proportions scattered in other fields. This concentration of visiting scholars is quite predictable, with the possible exception of the large proportion in the health sciences. It is possible to argue that the transition from an emphasis on barefoot doctors during the Cultural Revolution to having some 19 percent of the scholars in the United States doing advanced research in the medical field was too rapid and more responsive to the desires of individuals in the upper echelons of the medical profession than to the current needs of the society. However, Chinese medical

TABLE 5-25 Percentage Distribution of Funds Spent on PRC J-1 Research Scholars, by Source of Funds, 1979-1985

Source of Funds	1979	1980	1981	1982	1983	1984	1985
PRC government	64	51	44	42	37	30	23
Personal funds	2	4	4	4	5	6	8
U.S. government	1	6	5	7	7	7	7
U.S. university	19	30	36	37	39	42	48
U.S. foundation	3	3	2	2	3	3	3
U.S. corporation	0	--	--	--	--	--	--
International organization	2	1	1	1	2	2	1
Other	9	6	7	8	8	10	10
Total	100	100	100	100	100	100	100

NOTE: The symbol "--" indicates a value less than 0.5 percent.

SOURCE: USIA data tapes.

TABLE 5-26 Percentage Distribution of PRC J-1 Research Scholars Entering a New Program, by Field, 1979-1985

Field of Study	Year Program Began						
	1979	1980	1981	1982	1983	1984	1985
Agriculture	2	2	3	4	5	4	3
American studies	0	0	0	0	0	--	--
Architecture	--	1	--	--	--	--	--
Business management	--	--	1	2	1	2	2
Computer science	3	3	4	2	3	3	3
Education	--	2	1	2	1	2	2
Engineering	29	34	36	32	25	26	24
English as a second language (ESL)	0	1	--	1	--	1	1
Health sciences	9	11	12	13	19	17	19
Humanities	--	2	1	3	4	3	3
Law	--	--	--	1	1	2	2
Library and archival science	0	--	--	1	--	1	1
Life sciences	9	10	11	10	9	10	10
Mathematics	7	5	3	4	3	3	2
Physical sciences	35	25	22	21	22	17	21
Social sciences	3	3	4	4	5	8	5
Other or not stated	--	1	1	2	1	1	2
Total	100	100	100	100	100	100	100
(N)	(631)	(1,232)	(2,036)	(1,694)	(1,861)	(2,188)	(3,049)

NOTE: The symbol "--" indicates a value less than 0.5 percent.

SOURCE: USIA data tapes.

sciences are strong and are credited with a number of breakthroughs that have received international recognition; the 19 percent of the scholars who are in the health sciences translates to fewer than 600 individuals; and the medical schools in China are training large numbers of personnel to staff the health facilities that serve the daily needs of the public.

ESTIMATING THE NUMBER OF STUDENTS AND SCHOLARS IN THE UNITED STATES

Despite the considerable volume of statistics presented above, the much sought-after figure for the number of Chinese students and scholars in the United States in any given year continues to elude us, as it does the Chinese. What follows, then, is an effort to combine some of the hard data with impressions, anecdotal material, and

TABLE 5-27 Estimated Number of PRC Students and Scholars in the United States, 1979-1985

| Year | J-1 Visa | | | F-1 Visa | | | Est. Total in the United States by Year |
	New	Cont.	Total	New	Est. Cont.	Est. Total	
1979	891	134	1,025	523	0	523	1,548
1980	1,854	866	2,720	2,338	502	2,840	5,560
1981	3,210	2,358	5,568	2,341	2,631	4,972	10,540
1982	3,078	3,907	6,985	1,153	4,254	5,407	12,378
1983	3,882	5,897	9,779	1,003	4,188	5,191	12,931
1984	4,631	6,874	11,505	1,677	3,553	5,230	16,735
1985	6,340	6,559	12,899	3,001	3,478	6,479	19,378

NOTE: J-1 figures are based on USIA data tapes. They differ from those in Table 5-1 because USIA data are based on program years, while consular reports are for calendar years. The number of continuing F-1 students is estimated on the basis of "planned length of stay" entries on visa applications and is therefore a gross approximation.

perhaps common sense to come up with a usable estimate, or at least a point of departure for those who may wish to make alternate assumptions.

According to statistics assembled by the Department of State, we know that between 1979 and 1987 the United States issued about 62,000 J-1 and F-1 visas to citizens of the PRC (see Table 5-1). What we do not know is exactly how many of the recipients of these visas are in the country now or were here in any given year. Nevertheless, by separately analyzing the J-1 visas (responsibility of the USIA) and the F-1 visas (responsibility of the INS) some ballpark estimates can be made.

Since the USIA requires students and scholars holding J-1 visas to fill out a new IAP-66 form during each year that they remain in the United States, two separate numbers are available: one for new students and one for continuing students. By simply adding the two figures together, it is possible to obtain the total number of J-1 visa holders in the country in any specific year (see Table 5-27). Although these are, theoretically, the most accurate figures available, unfortunately they are not available after 1985. From Table 5-27 it can be seen that the number of J-1s increased rapidly during the early years (more than doubling from 1979 to 1980), but slowed sharply once large numbers of students and scholars started to return to

China. In 1985 there were approximately 13,000 Chinese students and scholars in the United States with J-1 visas.

Since we know the total number of J-1 visas issued and the number of J-1 students and scholars in the United States, then we must obviously know how many returned to China during each of the years under discussion. Referring to Table 5-27 again, subtracting the number of continuing students and scholars in a given year from the previous year's total, we obtain the following number of returnees:

1980:	159	1983:	1,088
1981:	362	1984:	2,905
1982:	1,661	1985:	4,946

In other words, from 1979 through 1985, about 11,000 (11,121) individuals with J-1 visas returned to China. Although the method does not exclude from the totals individuals who adjusted their status in the United States, these numbers have been very small and can be disregarded.[5] What cannot be disregarded, however, is that in addition to students and scholars, the J-1 visa holders include teachers (below the college level), trainees (usually sponsored by U.S. business or foundations), nonmatriculated visiting scholars, and other individuals who come here on a variety of exchange programs. The USIA estimates that this "other" category accounts for about 15 percent of the J-1 visas. Adjusting the 11,121 for the "other" category (automatically excluded from Chinese statistics on returnees), we reduce the number of J-1 returnees to about 9,500.

The real ambiguity starts after 1985. Although we know that in 1986 and 1987 approximately 16,000 Chinese students and scholars entered the United States on J-1 visas (see Table 5-1), we do not have the USIA data tapes that would make it possible to determine how many of those already in the country continued their education and how many returned to China after 1985. We do know, however, that despite a growing tendency to delay their return, many thousands

---

[5] According to the INS, the number of individuals converting from J-1 visas to permanent resident status was as follows: 1983: 43; 1984: 20; 1985: 50; 1986: 53; and 1987: 64.

TABLE 5-28 Summary of Estimates as of January 1988

| | Students and Scholars | | |
	J-1 Visas	F-1 Visas	Total
Visas issued to students and scholars (1979-1987)	34,000	22,000	56,000
Enrolled in degree program or doing research	21,000	7,000	28,000
Legally or illegally changed status to remain in U.S.	500	8,000	8,500
Returned to China	12,500	7,000	19,500

NOTE: See text for a discussion of sources of data and assumptions that produced these figures. Figures exclude trainees, teachers, and international visitors with J-1 visas.

of students, scholars, and short-term visitors continued to return to China during the two years. Taking all these facts into consideration, it is estimated that at the end of 1987 there were about 21,000 Chinese students and scholars in the United States with J-1 visas.[6]

Since there is no reliable way of keeping track of the activities of F-1 students once they come to the United States, any estimate of the number of privately sponsored Chinese students in this country is questionable. The figures in Table 5-26 are based on the "planned length of stay" information, which is entered by each individual on the visa application. As we know, however, for most F-1 students these entries are hypothetical. Although most indicate that they plan to remain in the United States for a minimum of two years and many plan to stay as long as four or five,[7] in fact, a large propor-

---

[6] If we reduce the 16,000 who entered this country in 1986–1987 with J-1 visas by 15 percent to eliminate the "others" in this category, we get a rounded 14,000 students and scholars. Reducing it further by an estimated 6,000 J-1s who returned to China in 1986 and 1987 (slightly lower than the average in the preceding two years), we are left with 8,000 students and scholars who, when added to the 13,000 who were already here in 1985, gives us a total of 21,000 students and scholars with J-1 visas.

[7] In 1985, for example, 37 percent of the F-1 visa applicants indicated a desire to spend 13 to 14 months in the United States, 21 percent planned to remain 25 to 36 months, and 20 percent indicated that they will stay 37 to 48 months.

tion extend their schooling or adjust their status to remain in this country indefinitely. In other words, when considering F-1s, a triple distinction has to be made between those who returned to China, those still in school, and those who remained in the United States, either by legally changing their status (before or after graduation) or hiding as undocumented residents.[8] The inclusion of F-1s in Table 5-27 is therefore only illustrative and a point of departure for the following, carefully considered yet speculative estimates: Of the 22,000 F-1 visas issued to Chinese students between 1979 and 1987, approximately one-third returned home, one-third are still in school, and one-third have managed to remain in the United States in a nonstudent capacity. All of the above conjectures are summarized in Table 5-28. To attempt more precision would be not only presumptuous but foolhardy.

---

[8] According to the INS, the number of F-1s who have adjusted to permanent resident status was: 1983: 1,163; 1984: 607; 1985: 739; 1986: 825; and 1987: 744, for a total of 4,078. By way of comparison, during the same time period, 7,648 individuals with F-1 visas from Taiwan adjusted to permanent status.

Conclusion
Chinese Students: An Emerging Issue in U.S.–China Relations?

From a rapprochement born primarily of security considerations, the United States and China have developed a friendly and multifarious relationship, which has evolved to include a great variety of economic, scientific, and intellectual interests in both countries. This does not mean that the relationship has not, at times, been strained. Some problems have come and gone while others, such as the seemingly eternal Taiwan issue, and the Congress-inspired tensions over China's family planning policies and human rights in Tibet, seem to have no immediate resolution and will continue to introduce some tension into U.S.–China relations. In a way, then, it is surprising that the decision of a large number of Chinese students to remain in the United States has not, at least so far, made an "unpleasant incident" list. The obvious question is whether this nagging and intensifying irritant—still to some extent soft-pedaled by the Chinese—is likely to turn into a more serious controversy in U.S.–China relations.

The loss to the United States of students who have completed their education in this country is not a problem unique to China. It has been a post-World War II phenomenon experienced by both developed and developing nations around the world. What then makes China more sensitive to this issue? Several answers can be suggested.

First, the most obvious reason. Still desperately striving to overcome the debilitating effects of the Cultural Revolution on China's education, the country needs all the high-level work force that it can train. Modernization and economic reforms have gone hand-in-hand with increased investments in education, and the nonreturn of students and scholars represents not only a significant loss of professionals but also of scarce funds. In China's case this problem is magnified, because whereas personal or family funds support two-thirds of the students coming to the United States from other nations, the proportion is reversed for China and two-thirds of her students are government sponsored, if not government funded. Although an ever-growing share of the cost of educating Chinese students is borne by American institutions, in just three years between 1983 and 1985 Beijing has spent some US$75 million on their nationals in the United States. Obviously, students who remain in the United States do not make a contribution to China's development and therefore do not compensate the nation for these outlays or, for that matter, the cost of their early upbringing and education.

In part, the gravity of the problem is also related to the rapidity with which it developed. In the case of other nations, the loss of college-educated professionals accelerated gradually and, on an annual basis, involved relatively modest numbers. In China's case, many tens of thousands of students and scholars were sent to this country in a period of less than a decade. Although China was admittedly prepared to suffer a loss of a small proportion of the graduates, the potential magnitude of people-loss now projected by some observers is much greater than Beijing bargained for. To make matters worse, many who are seeking to stay in the United States are the "top of the line" scholars, selected for foreign study by China's most prestigious scientific, academic, and government institutions. In other words, as anxious as Beijing is to see the return of all Chinese students, the problem has as much to do with the quality of students who remain behind as with their numbers. Between 1984 and 1986 PRC citizens earned 266 doctorates in science and engineering in U.S. universities,[1] and it is just these individuals who are most likely to extend their stay in the United States and seek ways to circumvent the visa legalities that force their return. As more and more Chinese enrolled in PhD programs in the sciences complete their studies, so will the concern over those who remain in the United States.

---

[1]National Science Foundation, *Science and Engineering Doctorates: 1960–86* (Washington, D.C.: National Science Foundation, 1988), NSF 88-309, p. 140.

Finally, the loss of students also involves "loss of face"—an especially painful condition for the Chinese. Anxiety about what this might communicate to the rest of the world about China—living and working conditions, professional opportunities available to her people, and, therefore, the viability of her system—is greatly accentuated by distress over the conclusions that might be drawn by the people in Taiwan and in the highly politicized Chinese community in the United States, whose support and goodwill Beijing seeks. Even so, the "loss of face" issue with regard to defecting students would not be nearly as vexing to the Chinese leadership were it not for the relatively small proportion of student activists who speak and write against their government and who are accused by Beijing of conducting "demagogical propaganda for counter-revolutionary ends." Since those who are promoting the sending of scholars abroad are already exposed politically, the loss of valuable people and the antigovernment activities by some are undoubtedly ammunition for opponents of the open door who, at a minimum, prefer not leaving it ajar.

All these are serious concerns for the Chinese government, but they cannot be blamed on U.S. policies or congressional resolutions; they must be resolved by the Chinese themselves. The question of why some Chinese scholars choose to stay in the United States was discussed in some detail in the body of this report. Briefly, the answer centers on inadequate compensation and generally poor living conditions in China; on the residual mistrust of intellectuals, recurrent intrusions of the state into the lives of individuals, and the related political considerations; and, for scientific personnel, China's inability to provide them with facilities, equipment, and projects that will challenge and satisfy their professional abilities and ambitions. It is not unreasonable to generalize that Chinese scholars with U.S. PhD degrees aspire to do basic research in an institute of the Chinese Academy of Sciences, rather than work in a production enterprise. Given China's current policies and capabilities, however, relatively few returning scientists can be accommodated in this way. Although there continue to be important pockets of basic research throughout the scientific establishment, the current emphasis is clearly on applied research and development—on the linking of research with production. Even the President of the Chinese Academy of Sciences, after a prescribed nod toward basic research, proclaimed that "the main scientific and technological force" of the Academy must be sent "to the main battlefield of serving economic construction."[2]

---

[2]Zhou Guangzhao, "The Chinese Academy of Sciences Advances in the

And now that the responsibility system, which started in the countryside in the early 1980s, has come to the scientific establishment, and most research and development funding (excluding mathematics and certain fields within the physical and biological sciences) must come from contractual agreements and consultations with production enterprises, opportunities in basic research for the thousands of returning scientists will be scarce indeed. Beijing's current effort to arrange for students to obtain practical experience while abroad makes sense in terms of the country's present needs, but in the case of students who are already here, it is targeting individuals whose original goals and training would make them reluctant participants. In sum, to reduce the numbers of students choosing to remain in the United States, China must make their return economically and professionally more attractive.

There are other aspects to the student defection problem, however, for which the U.S. side can share at least some of the responsibility. Beijing believes that not enough is being done by the various government agencies—from the Immigration and Naturalization Service to the U.S. Information Agency—to force Chinese nationals to comply with existing regulations and return home as scheduled. In theory, Chinese representatives understand that federal officials will neither dictate to academic and research institutions on their handling of Chinese students nor insist that special procedures, not applied to other foreign students, be introduced. In fact, it is difficult for the Chinese to see why unique circumstances and serious concerns of a friendly nation cannot be given special consideration, and they have requested at several high-level meetings that U.S. immigration laws be tightened.[3] They suspect that much has to do with U.S. desires to appropriate China's most promising people.

In less than one decade, Chinese students have made a significant impact on U.S. institutions of higher education. University administrators involved in international student affairs resist making generalizations on the basis of student citizenship, but privately will confide that while Chinese students cause the greatest frustrations

---

Course of Reforms," *Renmin Ribao* (*Peoples Daily*), March 28, 1987; FBIS, April 6, 1987, pp. K27–31.

[3] The French government, for example, has pleased the Chinese by a recent proclamation that France will not support the tendency of Chinese students to stay and work in that country and that government-sponsored students must return home after finishing their studies (Xinhua, Feb. 25, 1988; FBIS-CHI-88-041, March 2, 1988, p. 10).

and take the most time, they also make a very positive impression and are an especially valuable addition to the U.S. academic community. This perception is even more prevalent among professors, especially those in science and engineering, who have come to place great reliance on the competitive, intelligent, and hard-working students from China. In the course of the last several years, and despite language handicaps, Chinese PhD candidates and postdoctoral students have become qualified and highly attractive research and teaching assistants, and U.S. professors have come to depend greatly on them in sustaining many important programs. It should also be noted that with a serious shortage of U.S. graduate students, especially in fields of engineering, the Chinese are filling a recognized need.

It would seem, then, the contention of Chinese officials that some U.S. professors and researchers try to entice Chinese students in science and technology to remain in this country, is not entirely without substance. Very likely some are doing just that, ignoring the appeals of Chinese officials to "work together" to assure the return of students. Nor is it an exaggeration to say that, for the most part, the attraction between Chinese students and their U.S. professors is mutual.

It is easy to sympathize with Chinese concerns and as the number of Chinese students and scholars in the United States increases, so does the speculation as to how Beijing plans to address this problem. The latest spate of rumors about China's future plans for foreign study were precipitated by a State Education Commission document, which was published on November 28, 1987, but did not become public knowledge for several months. The directive set limits on the number of years a student can spend in the United States: one to two years for a master's degree, five years for a student with a bachelor's degree, and four years for a student with a master's degree seeking a doctorate.[4] These new time limits provoked an open letter to Premier Li Peng, signed by hundreds of Chinese students in U.S. universities. It was a long and cordial letter that listed all the reasons why time limits are unreasonable, pointed out that it is in China's interest for the students to take full advantage of the academic and financial resources available to them in this country, and concluded with the hope that the leaders will "prevent further disharmony" by

---

[4]See, for example, Denis Hevesi, "China Policy Shift on Study Overseas," *New York Times,* April 8, 1988, p. A5.

re-examining the policies for overseas study and making appropriate adjustments.

Although the November directive said nothing specific about reducing the number of students sent to the United States, it resulted in a number of articles in the U.S. press predicting drastic cuts on the basis of a misinterpretation of a statement that the number of *"state-sponsored"* students sent here will be limited to 20 percent.[5] This brought quick denials by the Chinese government. The Xinhua news agency published an interview with Huang Xinbai, a member of the State Education Commission who is in charge of the foreign-study program, in which he affirmed that China's policy of sending students abroad has not changed and that rumors of cuts were groundless and "fabricated with ulterior motives."[6] Huang further disclosed that in 1988, 4,600 students will be sent to the United States, of which 600 will be state-funded and 4,000 will be financed by various institutions and departments. Others will continue to come as self-financed students.

There is no reason to doubt Chinese assurances that thousands of their students and scholars will continue to come to the United States. China acknowledges that foreign education is still vital to her modernization plans and that U.S. institutions have the wherewithal to provide training and research experience unmatched elsewhere in the world. From the perspective of the scholar, and despite conflicting and fluctuating images, the United States continues to be the country of choice and the idea of coming here still evokes a subtle sensory stimulus unmatched by other countries. It is also no small matter that courses are taught in English, the *lingua franca* every Chinese student wants to master. The flow of Chinese students and scholars would not have persisted if this country did not meet academic expectations, furnish opportunities for financial support for study and research, and provide (with the help of a large Chinese community) a congenial environment. That is why sporadic efforts to send a larger proportion of scholars to Europe and Japan has never met with enthusiasm or success.

Under the circumstances, it may not be too outlandish to suggest

---

[5] See, for example, Fox Butterfield, "China Plans to Let Fewer Students Go Abroad, Especially to the U.S.," *New York Times,* March 24, 1988, p. A1.

[6] *CD*, April 7, 1988; also published as a special press release by the Chinese Embassy, Washington, D.C.

that any serious restriction on the opportunity to study in American institutions of higher education might precipitate a repeat of the winter of 1986–1987 student demonstrations and even adversely affect the morale of the younger generation—both undergraduates and those still in secondary schools. More important, policy restrictions and the possible reaction to them on the home front would be completely counterproductive in terms of inducing Chinese scholars still in the United States to return home. Certainly the arrest, trial, and conviction of Yang Wei, who completed his graduate work at the University of Arizona, for writing articles attacking Chinese policies while in the United States aroused serious concerns among Chinese students abroad and at home.[7]

Tight controls over the sending of scholars to the United States would also have broader implications of considerable consequence for Beijing. Any such restrictions would send the wrong message to the outside world and once again raise questions with regard to the sincerity of China's open-door policy. This could quickly create diplomatic tensions that might spill over, not only into such vital areas as commercial ventures and the acquisition of technology, but also into routine but important contacts that now exist between the academic and research communities of the two countries.

If we take China at her word, she hopes to minimize the likelihood of losing future students to the United States, not so much by reducing their numbers as by changing the qualifications and characteristics of those going abroad. Accepting the recommendations of Chinese scholars and officials who had looked into this problem over the years, Beijing will strive to limit foreign education, especially in the United States, to PhD and postdoctoral levels. Consequently, most of the new entrants to U.S. universities will have spent several years working or doing research at home, and their study and research abroad will be closely tied to the needs of their work unit. In other words, many more will stay in the United States for shorter periods of time and know exactly what they will be returning to. Considering China's mixed record of implementing announced policies, we can only wait to see how closely this one will be followed and how many resourceful Chinese youths will find ways to circumvent it.

In the meantime, certain changes have occurred on the U.S. side,

---

[7]See, for example, *CD*, Dec. 22, 1987, p. 3.

which may (unwittingly) facilitate China's implemention of the new regulations. There are now more Chinese students in the United States than all other nationals studying here. Not only has the novelty worn off, but also many universities believe that students from China are already overrepresented on their campuses—often at the expense of U.S. and other foreign students. There also seems to be a decreasing amount of funding available for Chinese students. In some cases this reflects overall cuts in scholarship money; in other cases, specific departments that already have a number of Chinese graduate students are reluctant to add more before some of their compatriots complete their studies and leave. These factors and perhaps an unspoken U.S. desire to decrease the flow of Chinese students to this country may explain reports by some recent arrivals that although the lines in front of the U.S. Embassy and Consulates in China are as long as ever, visa officials are becoming more cautious and vigilant, and student visas are more difficult to obtain.

Without in any way minimizing China's dilemma with regard to the loss of scholars, it is nevertheless important to consider to what extent students who remain in the United States undermine the goals of both modernization and the exchange program? Setting aside the issues of "loss of face" and possible political backlash, and viewing the problem from the long-term strategic, commercial, and humanistic perspective, it is quite possible to conclude that, on balance, China's loss of a certain proportion of students should be neither a "complete loss" nor a national crisis.

Based on the experience of Chinese immigrants who came here in earlier decades, as well as conversations with more recent arrivals, ties with the motherland are not easily broken. Short-term disillusionment tends to pass with time, while long-term pride and good will toward China (if not toward the current regime) endures. Given the opportunity by Beijing, the young people will maintain contacts with family and friends, will return for visits, and will share much of what they have learned and the experience they have acquired with their colleagues at home. Graduates of U.S. universities who return to China and those who remain in the United States combine to increase the understanding between the two countries and can be invaluable in establishing both formal and informal lines of communications between their scientific, industrial, and even political establishments. In other words, students are not only "carriers of culture" (a possible minus), but also carriers of technical know-how (an indisputable plus). U.S.-educated Chinese intellectuals already serve as an important and multifaceted bridge in U.S.–China relations, and as they mature and advance, their positive influence will only increase.

Besides, China's current brain drain is not necessarily permanent. If China continues on the road to modernization, the inevitable changes in the society will make the country more attractive to intellectuals who have been exposed to individual, economic, and professional freedoms and will prompt many of them to return. Others may become homesick, disillusioned with the United States, or both. Whether they return in three, five, or more years, they will naturally be much better equipped to make important contributions to China's development.

In the final analysis, both Washington and Beijing must look at the present and potential issues raised by the defection of scholars from a much broader national perspective of self-interest. If an economically and politically healthy China is in the interests of the United States—and most believe it is—and if close and friendly relations with the United States are in the long-term interest of China—and most believe they are—then, however Beijing decides to approach the problem of Chinese students who choose to remain in the United States, this issue should not become a major bone of contention in U.S.–China relations.

Appendix

State Education Commission Provisions on Study Abroad

STATE EDUCATION COMMISSION ISSUES
PROVISIONS ON STUDY ABROAD

Beijing, XINHUA Domestic Service in Chinese, 10 June 87. Translated in JPRS-CAR-87-024, July 23, 1987, pp. 89–99.

(Text) Beijing, 10 June (XINHUA)—With the approval of the party Central Committee and the State Council, the State Education Commission recently decided to make public "Certain Interim Provisions of the State Education Commission on the Work of Sending Personnel To Study Abroad."

The CPC Central Committee and the State Council last year specifically discussed the work of sending personnel to study abroad. The party Central Committee and the State Council hold that since the 3rd Plenary Session of the 11th CPC Central Committee, China has made great achievements in sending personnel to study abroad in various forms, and the practice must be firmly continued in the future because it completely conforms to our long-term policy of opening to the outside world. In order to make the work of sending personnel to study abroad meet the needs of our country's Four Modernizations, the party Central Committee and the State Council have instructed the departments concerned and the Chinese Embassies and Consulates abroad to actively improve the work on the principle of summing up experience, promoting what is beneficial, and eliminating what is harmful. They have also entrusted the State Education Commission with the work of sending personnel to study abroad.

Following the instructions of the party Central Committee and the State Council, the State Education Commission has formulated certain interim provisions on the work of sending personnel to study abroad and begun to implement the provisions since December last year. The contents of the provisions are as follows:

I.   Guiding Principles for the Work of Sending Personnel To Study Abroad

1. To send Chinese citizens to study in institutions of higher learning and research organizations in foreign countries through various channels and in various forms is a component part of China's policy of opening to the outside world. The practice is an important way to learn advanced science and technology, applicable economic and administrative management experience, and other useful knowledge from foreign countries, and to train our highly specialized personnel. It helps develop friendship and exchanges between the Chinese people and the people of other countries. Therefore, we must continue, for a long time to come, the practice of sending personnel to study abroad in various forms in a planned way to meet the needs of our building socialist material and spiritual civilizations.

2. The work of sending personnel to study abroad should consider the realities of our socialist modernization program and meet the needs of our domestic production and construction, scientific research, and personnel training so as to solve the important questions concerning scientific research and production and enhance our ability to train highly specialized personnel.

3. The work of sending personnel to study abroad should be done on the principle of learning the strong points of foreign countries. While we must study basic sciences as well as applied science and engineering, emphasis should be placed on the latter at present.

Attention should be paid to the needs of developing our country's vocational and technical education.

4. Personnel should be sent to study abroad according to needs; quality should be ensured; study should be coordinated with application; management and education of personnel studying abroad should be improved; and efforts should be made to create the necessary conditions for personnel studying abroad to apply what they have learned and play a positive role in China's socialist modernization after they return home.

5. Personnel studying abroad must abide by the relevant laws and regulations of China as well as the laws of the country where they study. They must respect the customs, habits, and religious beliefs of the host country.

II. Management of Work of Sending Personnel to Study Abroad

1. The State Education Commission, working under the leadership of the State Council in accordance with the principles and policies of sending personnel to study abroad by the state, is in charge of the work of sending personnel to study abroad, and placement after their return home. Planning for sending personnel of non-educational departments to study abroad and their placement after their return shall be the joint responsibility of the State Scientific and Technological Commission and the State Economic Commission working in accordance with unified principles and policies.

2. Adhering to the principle of simplifying administrative procedures and delegating powers to lower-level units, the state will control only a portion of the personnel to be sent to study abroad and will allocate the rest to employing organizations. After conducting experiments at selected organizations, the organization that sends personnel to study abroad shall gradually take the responsibility of controlling funds earmarked for study abroad and maintaining spending within the authorized amount.

3. Units sending personnel to study abroad should appoint a specialized organization or specialized personnel to keep in touch with

the personnel sent, guiding their study abroad and actively coordinating with and assisting Chinese Embassies and Consulates in administering the affairs concerning personnel studying abroad.

4. Successful administration of the affairs concerning personnel studying abroad is an important task of the Chinese Embassies and Consulates. The educational section (group) of the embassy or consulate dispatched by the State Education Commission and the cadres appointed by the embassy or consulate to administer the affairs concerning personnel studying abroad shall work under the leadership of the embassy or consulate to handle the specific tasks in administering the affairs concerning these personnel during the period of their study abroad.

5. The educational section (group) of the embassy or consulate or cadres in charge of administering the affairs concerning personnel studying abroad as well as the departments and units sending the personnel abroad should show concern for the personnel sent, help them resolve difficulties or problems encountered, keep them informed of the country's developments and needs, and enthusiastically serve them. Embassies and consulates should carry out education in patriotism, collectivism, and socialist ideas and ethics among the personnel studying abroad and help strengthen their faith in revitalizing China through hard work.

6. "Student associations," "friendship associations," and other groups formed by personnel studying abroad are mass organizations through which personnel studying abroad will educate themselves, administer their own affairs, and provide services for the members.

7. Departments at home responsible for administering the affairs of personnel studying abroad and departments and units sending the personnel abroad should promptly make job arrangements for personnel returning from their study abroad to ensure that they can fully display their role.

III. Selection of Personnel Studying Abroad on Government Programs

1. Personnel studying abroad on government programs refers to persons systematically, and through various means, sent abroad for

study in accordance with the needs of China's development; they are funded, either wholly or partly, by the state or the relevant departments, localities, or units.

Persons who are selected nationwide uniformly according to state plans and who are sent abroad on funds falling under the category of uniform expenditures are called "personnel studying abroad on state programs" ("state program personnel" for short). Persons who are selected from a given locality or unit according to the plans of the department, locality, or unit and who are sent abroad on funds falling under the category of the department, locality, or unit expenditure (including those who have the approval and support of the units they work for, have received scholarships, loans, or financial aid, and are incorporated in the plan for personnel studying abroad) are called "personnel studying abroad on department, locality, or unit programs" ("unit program personnel" for short).

2. Personnel studying abroad on government programs can be divided into undergraduate students, graduate students, advanced studies personnel, and visiting scholars.

Normally, the period of study abroad for regular or professional undergraduates and graduate students shall be decided by the units sending them abroad in accordance with the academic system of the host country. The period of study for advanced studies personnel and visiting scholars shall normally range from 3 to 12 months, as dictated by the actual needs of the advanced studies and research; in extraordinary circumstances, it can last 18 months. In any case, the units sending the personnel abroad shall decide the length of stay in accordance with their own plans.

4. Units sending personnel abroad should help and guide the personnel in the selection of the institutions for study and for doing practical work or research. The selected institutions should have a fairly high academic standard or be strong in a given field.

5. Qualifications of personnel studying abroad on government programs:

(1) Political Qualifications

They must be personnel who ardently love the motherland and socialism; have good ideological and moral qualities; have distinguished themselves in practical work and study; and have actively served socialist modernization.

(2) Vocational Qualifications
Personnel studying abroad as undergraduates should be high school graduates with outstanding academic records. Personnel studying abroad as graduates should have graduated from college or higher educational institutions with outstanding academic records and should have work experience prior to their departure for abroad. The length of their practical work shall be decided in accordance with the characteristics of their discipline. Personnel going abroad for advanced studies or as visiting scholars should be backbone professional personnel engaged in teaching, research, or production, having graduated from colleges or higher educational institutions and having worked in their special field at institutions of higher learning, research units, or industrial or mining enterprises for more than five years (the period may be appropriately shortened if the personnel are extremely outstanding or if the work requirements so dictate), or persons holding master's degrees engaged in their special field of work or in vocational or technical educational work for more than two years. The age limit for advanced studies personnel and visiting scholars should be set according to the nature of their studies and research. Generally, their age should not be over 50. The age limit may be appropriately eased for visiting scholars at or above associate professor or research fellow level who go abroad for a short period (three to six months).

(3) Foreign Language Requirements
Personnel studying abroad should have a good command of the language of the host country. They should be able to read professional books and periodicals in the foreign language with relative ease; to comprehend, speak, and write the foreign language to a certain degree; and to carry out academic exchanges in the foreign language after a short period of training. Personnel studying abroad as undergraduates should be able to receive lectures in the foreign language.

(4) Physical Conditions
The health of the personnel going abroad for study on government programs must conform with health criteria for personnel studying

abroad; health certificates (valid for one year) must be obtained from hospitals at the provincial and municipal levels.

6. Selection of personnel studying abroad on government programs:

(1) The State Education Commission shall decide on the number and category of the state program personnel and the proportion among various destination countries and various disciplines and shall arrange for their selection. The department, localities, or units sending personnel abroad to study shall decide on the number and category of the unit program personnel and the proportion among various destination countries and between various disciplines and shall arrange for their selection in accordance with the general guidelines of the State Education Commission for the Record through the responsible departments.

(2) Advanced studies personnel and visiting scholars studying abroad on government programs shall be selected through a process involving recommendation by the unit, evaluation by the academic organization or technological department, review (check) by the personnel department, and approval by the leadership.

(3) Personnel studying abroad as undergraduates or graduates on government programs shall be selected through a process combining examination and overall evaluation of the personnel's moral, intellectual, and physical standards.

7. Signing an "agreement on studying abroad":

(1) Prior to the formalities for going abroad, personnel on government programs shall sign an "agreement on studying abroad" between sending units and the personnel leaving for study abroad and have it publicly notarized.

(2) The contents of the "agreement on studying abroad" must specify the objectives, subjects, and length of required service at home after studying abroad; expenses to be provided to personnel studying; and rights, obligations, and responsibilities of the sending unit and the personnel sent to study abroad.

8. Preparation and intensive training of personnel going to study abroad on government programs:

Prior to the personnel departing for study abroad, the sending unit should adopt various forms of short-term intensive training programs to help the personnel be prepared ideologically. The intensive training program should include: principles and policies of foreign affairs, regulations governing personnel studying abroad, foreign laws, introduction to conditions in the host countries, and other appropriate matters.

9. Regulations governing wages, seniority, and management of expenses incurred:

(1) During the approved period of studying abroad of the personnel and visiting scholars, their wages will continue to be issued by the original units and their seniority will also be protected. For graduates sent abroad on doctorate programs, the period of their study abroad will be counted as equivalent in seniority at home after they obtain their degrees. As for those employed personnel who are sent abroad to study, their wages at home during their studying abroad will be handled in accordance with the regulations governing personnel who are in the same category.

(2) The expenses of personnel sent by the state to study abroad, such as clothing purchase fees, travel expenses, tuition, and living expenses during their study abroad, and round-trip expenses for graduates and undergraduates to vacation at home during their studies, shall be handled according to the unified state regulations.

(3) The expenses of the personnel sent by units to study abroad, such as clothing purchase fees, travel expenses, tuition, and living expenses for graduates and undergraduates during their studies, shall be handled according to stipulated regulations, and in accordance with the specific conditions of the sending units coupled with unified state regulations governing the sending department, locality, and unit.

10. Personnel sent to study abroad should study hard and return home to serve the country as planned. During or after their study

abroad, the personnel in general must not change their student status. If there is a need for them to extend their stay, they should submit their application to the original sending unit for approval ahead of time. During their extended period of studying abroad, their wages at home should be issued by the original unit as before. As for those who, without official approval, do not return home as scheduled the extension will be held as leave without pay for the first year. After one year, whether their posts shall be reserved will depend on decisions of the sending units regarding the various conditions.

11. The State Education Commission will be in charge of expenses required to send personnel to study abroad by the state and provide guidance for regulating and managing expenses of studying abroad to the sending departments, localities, and units. The specific management of expenses of the personnel sent to study abroad by the state shall be taken care of by special officials of the education department (section) of an embassy or a consulate or shall be handled by the financial department of an embassy or consulate.

IV. Engaging in Postdoctorate Research or Practical Training Abroad:

1. The subjects on which postdoctorate research are done or training received should be able to facilitate development of China's science and technology.

2. Those who engage in postdoctorate research are in two categories: (a) those with doctorate degrees who have been employed at home may apply to do postdoctorate research abroad; and (b) those graduates studying abroad who have obtained doctorate degrees may apply to do postdoctorate research immediately afterward.

Receiving practical training abroad means that after obtaining their master's or doctorate degrees, the graduate students receive short-term training in a company or an enterprise without changing their student status.

3. Regulations governing examination and approval of those who are employed at home and apply to do postdoctorate research or receive such practical training abroad:

(1) The applicant should submit a report of application to the employing unit explaining reasons, subject matters, and time of the projected postdoctorate research or practical training.

(2) The employing unit should organize a group of experts and professors to examine the objectives of proposed postdoctorate research or the work scope of such practical training and give their opinions. After approval by responsible officials of the unit, the application should then be transmitted to the pertinent department of ministry or commission, province, autonomous region, or municipality—depending on which administration it belongs to—for examination of and approval for proceeding to formalities for going abroad.

(3) Expenses required for the postdoctorate research or practical training abroad should be covered by the sending unit.

(4) Those who are chosen for doing postdoctorate research or receiving practical training abroad will still be issued wages despite their absence at home.

4. Regulations governing examination of and approval for applications for doing postdoctorate research or receiving practical training abroad directly submitted by graduates just receiving degrees abroad:

(1) Applicant should submit a report to the original sending unit and Chinese Embassy or Consulate abroad ahead of time explaining reasons for, and subject matter and time of, the projected postdoctorate research program and practical training.

(2) Within three months after receipt of the application, the sending unit at home should organize a group of experts and professors to examine and give their opinions on the proposal. After approval by the responsible official of the unit, the applicant will be notified of the results by the embassy or consulate abroad. If no reply is received from the sending unit after three months, the decision will be made by the Chinese Embassy or Consulate abroad.

(3) After the applicant has made proper arrangements with and received a letter of appointment from the foreign institute where he/she will do the postdoctorate work or receive practical training,

he/she should personally inform the sending unit at home and the Chinese Embassy or Consulate abroad of the objectives of the postdoctorate research or work scope of the practical training, where the postdoctorate program is to be conducted, and the time needed. If the research topic or practice work scope is different from that specified in the application, a new application should be submitted for examination and approval.

(4) All expenses required for the postdoctorate research or training period and traveling expenses for returning home after completing the postdoctorate program will be borne by the applicant.

(5) Those who wish to be transferred to a third country for postdoctorate research or training after they have obtained their doctorate degrees abroad should submit their application for such purpose after having worked at home for a certain period of time. If one needs to be transferred to a third country from abroad due to some special reason, the application should be submitted six months in advance to the pertinent department of a ministry or commission, province, autonomous region, or municipality—depending on which administration it belongs to—for approval.

(6) The duration of a postdoctorate research or training program generally ranges from one to one-and-a-half years.

V. Home Leave for Personnel Studying Abroad and Spouse Visitation

1. Home leave for personnel studying abroad and visitation of their spouses abroad should be geared to helping the personnel understand the needs for and development of national construction projects, paying due attention to learning and living conditions of the personnel, and taking into consideration the working pattern of the units concerned at home.

2. As for those who are sent abroad on undergraduate and doctorate programs with a specified time of more than three years, they will enjoy a paid home leave after two years studying abroad. (During this time, the graduates of doctorate programs should have obtained the PhD candidate qualification.)

3. A person who is qualified for paid home leave should apply to a Chinese Embassy or Consulate abroad by him/herself according to certain regulations and return home via a designated route.

4. Applications for home leave paid by undergraduates and graduates studying abroad themselves can be submitted to a Chinese Embassy or Consulate abroad for examination and approval on the condition that it will not affect their studies.

5. During the period of their paid or self-paid home leave vacations, the funds enjoyed by the state or sending units will be stopped. As for their living expenses at home, they will be arranged by the sending unit in accordance with unified state regulations concerning the matter, coupled with certification from a Chinese Embassy or Consulate abroad.

6. The length of the home leave of the undergraduates and graduates studying abroad depends on the length of school vacations.

7. Since the time of studying abroad for the graduate students is relatively longer, the application of their spouses for visiting them abroad should be handled according to the "Regulations Governing Exit and Entry of Citizens of the People's Republic of China." If the spouse of the graduate sent to study abroad is currently employed, he/she should apply to the employing unit for visitation leave. With the approval of the employing unit, the visitation leave normally ranges from three to six months. Wages for the first 3 months will still be issued; the fourth to sixth months will be leave without pay; from the seventh month on, whether the post will be reserved depends on the decision of the employing unit.

If, during the visiting period, the spouse of the graduate student has obtained foreign scholarships or subsidiary funding and applies for studying abroad she/he can report to her/his employing unit for approval during her/his visitation abroad, thus becoming a public- or self-funded student studying abroad through proper procedure.

8. If the spouse of a graduate student sent to study abroad on government programs is the graduating student or postgraduate student of an institution of higher learning in China still pursuing her/his studies, generally speaking, no leave for visiting relatives abroad will

be approved in order to not interrupt her/his studies and research program.

9. Personnel sent to pursue advanced study abroad on government programs, and visiting scholars, according to regulations, are not entitled to home leave because the duration of their stay abroad is relatively short. Generally speaking, no leave for visiting relatives abroad will be granted to their spouses in China either, if the spouses are on-the-job employees.

VI. Studying Abroad at One's Own Expense

1. We should support those who go abroad for study at their own expense as it is a way of training talented personnel for national construction. Politically, they should be treated the same, without discrimination, as those personnel studying abroad on government programs. We should show concern for them, take good care of them, and encourage them to complete their studies at an early date and then return home to dedicate themselves to socialist modernization of the motherland.

2. Personnel going abroad for studying at their own expense refers to those Chinese citizens who have reliable proof that they can study or pursue advanced studies at foreign institutions of higher learning or scientific research institutions with financial support from their relatives and friends residing abroad or in Hong Kong, Macao, or Taiwan; or with the foreign exchange of their own or of their relatives and friends in China.

3. Those personnel who are not on the job; undergraduates of institutions of higher learning; returned overseas Chinese and their dependents; the dependents in China of overseas Chinese; Hong Kong, Macao, and Taiwan compatriots; and Chinese of foreign nationality are eligible for application to study abroad at their own expense so long as they conform to the stipulations of article 2 and have obtained admission to a foreign school and the financial guarantee.

4. In order to ensure a smooth order of work at institutions of higher learning, scientific research institutions, and other units in China, their employees requesting to leave their posts and pursue study

abroad at their own expense must obtain prior approval from their employing units.

Graduating students of the institutions of higher learning who have been included in the state assignment plan should accept the assignment and serve for the country.

Graduate students in China must endeavor to complete their studies and research program in accordance with the regulations governing their status as students. Generally, they are not allowed to interrupt their studies to go abroad for study at their own expense.

5. Application for studying abroad at their own expense by backbone specialized and technical personnel should be treated as cases of "state program personnel" as much as possible. They include assistant research fellows, lecturers, engineers, physicians-in-charge, personnel of higher positions, graduate students who have obtained their master's degrees, outstanding writers and artists, outstanding athletes, backbone office staff, and personnel having special skills or talents. During the period of study abroad, they shall be treated as "state program personnel" with regard to management abroad and wages at home.

6. Undergraduates of institutions of higher learning who have obtained approval to study abroad at their own expense may retain their status as a student for one year. On-the-job personnel who have obtained approval to study abroad at their own expense may retain their public office for one year, but their wages will be suspended, beginning in the month before the month of their departure.

7. When on-the-job personnel return to work in China after having completed their self-funded study abroad, their length of service prior to departure may be retained and calculated in addition to the work period after their return. For those who have obtained a doctorate degree abroad, their length of service in China is calculated in the same way as that for the "state program personnel."

8. Prior to departure of the personnel going abroad for study at their own expense, the units of these personnel and departments in charge of education of the ministries, commissions, provinces, autonomous regions, and municipalities concerned should brief them

on regulations concerning study abroad and relevant situations at home and abroad, and guide them in making arrangements for study abroad.

9. After those personnel going abroad for study at their own expense have arrived in foreign countries, they should report to and keep in touch with the Chinese Embassies and Consulates there. The Chinese Embassies and Consulates abroad, as well as the departments concerned at home, should also take the initiative to maintain contact with those who study abroad at their own expense, protect their legitimate interests and rights, encourage them to study hard, and show concern for their life and study abroad.

10. The international traveling expenses for the return trip of those who have studied abroad at their own expense, have obtained a bachelor's or higher degree, and are coming back to work in China shall be borne by the state or the employing units. The employing units shall provide their families at home with allowances according to their situations.

11. Chinese students studying abroad at their own expense who are graduating from graduate schools or are completing regular or specialized undergraduate courses there may ask for a job assignment from the state by contacting Chinese Embassies and Consulates six months before their graduation to process the relevant registration, so that the State Education Commission may arrange their job assignment. They may also register with the State Education Commission after their return to China. In this case, their application will be processed in accordance with the regulations governing job assignment and wage standards for "state program personnel" under the same category.

Where previously promulgated regulations governing study abroad contravene these regulations, they are superseded by these regulations.

Index

A

Academic exchanges
  assurance of continuation of, 8
  with Canada and European
      countries, 80
  effects of student demonstrations
      on, 1–2, 3
  disciplinary emphasis in, 13, 30,
      124–125
  importance to China, 27, 32, 36,
      52, 115, 119, 124
  of language students, 21
  modernization of China through,
      22–24
  national work conference in China,
      25–26
  and PRC-U.S. relations, 20–21, 23,
      114–122
  obstacles to, 23
  policy evolution in China on, 19–35
  post-Mao resumption of, 22–25
  purpose, 22–24
  risks to China, 36; *see also* Brain
      drain
  selection process, 30
  Sino-Soviet, 20
  "spiritual pollution" from, 2, 67

Accord for Educational Exchanges,
    23
Agreement on Cooperation in
    Science and Technology, 23

B

Beijing Languages Institute, 27
Brain drain
  international perspective on, 53–56
  official fears about, 14
  of officially sponsored
      students/scholars, 38–39
  of privately sponsored students,
      39–42
  projected magnitude of, 115
  prospects for, 49–52
  significance to China, 114, 122
  during Sino-Soviet academic
      exchanges, 20
  student perspectives on reasons for,
      42–49
  studies of, 53–54
  see also Emigration/delayed returns
      of students

C

Chinese Academy of Sciences, 24, 46, 60, 116
Chinese students abroad
  attitudes about professional goals, 5, 28, 37
  "bourgeois liberalization of," 3–4, 8
  characteristics of, 8, 11, 14, 23–24, 26, 30, 37–39, 42, 47, 62, 64, 65, 84–85, 95–100
  Chinese statistics on, 77–81, 101; *see also* Statistics on Chinese students
  contracts/agreements with work units, 30, 73, 129
  demands of, 2, 32
  effect of student demonstrations on, 4–5, 13–14, 120
  estimation of numbers of, 109–113
  family/spouse visits to, 96, 133–135
  funding of, 11, 27, 29, 31, 37, 46, 85–86, 90–91, 94–95, 97–98, 115, 121, 125
  graduates, 24, 27, 30, 41
  language proficiency, 24–25, 28–29, 43, 128
  limiting to PhD candidates and postdoctoral students, 37; *see also* Regulation of foreign study
  national qualifying examinations, 25
  origins of, 11, 92–93
  oversight by Chinese embassy/consular officials, 8, 50, 126
  perspectives on returning or emigrating, 42–49
  preference for U.S., 119–120
  preferential treatment by U.S. universities, 24–25
  qualifications of, 23, 25, 127–129
  researchers/scholars, *see* Research/visiting scholars
  selection process in China, 26, 27–28, 30, 38, 49, 49–50, 118–119, 126–131, 132
  sensitivity to rumors, 33
  undergraduates, 24, 27, 40
  see also Emigration/delayed returns of students/scholars; Returning

students/scholars; Student demonstrations; Visas/visa holders, F-1; Visas/visa holders, J-1
Cultural Revolution, 5, 23, 24, 47, 95, 108, 114–115

D

Deng Xiaoping, 4, 36
Dissidents, *see* Intellectual dissent/dissidents
Domestic graduates/scholars
  complaints of, 65–68
  tension between foreign-trained graduates/scholars, 58
  wages, 66
  see also PhDs, Chinese

E

Emigration/delayed returns of students/scholars
  benefits to China of, 52, 56, 121–122
  control of, 8, 13, 14, 55, 120
  effect on U.S.-China relations, 114
  of F-1 visa holders, 4, 9, 39, 40, 112–113
  facilitating factors, 46, 49, 119
  fears of Chinese officials, 4
  host country encouragement of, 70–71
  impediments to, 44–45, 96
  loss-of-face issue, 116
  of privately sponsored students, 4, 9, 39, 40, 112–113
  quality of students, 115
  reasons for, 44–45, 48–49, 54–56, 116
  U.S. attitudes and responsibility, 8–9, 117–118
  see also Brain drain

F

Fang Lizhi, 2
Fields of study
  Chinese developmental requirements/priorities, 15, 30, 33, 50, 71, 100, 120, 124, 131
  choice in, 100

gender differences in, 96
languages, 21
preferences, 11, 103–104
by type of visa, 11–13, 100–104

G

Gao Yi, 26
Graduate Record Examination, 25
Great Leap Forward, 20

H

He Dongchang, 8, 37, 71
Hu Yaobang, 1, 2
Huang Xinbai, 32–33

I

Intellectual dissent/dissidents
dismissals of intellectuals for, 1, 5
income and living conditions, 45–46
official reaction to, 3–4, 116, 120
student demands, 2, 32

J

Job assignments/opportunities
back door tactics for enticing
graduates in China, 59–60
in basic research, 117
basis for, 50
choice in, 59, 68–69
complaints of returning
students/scholars about, 14–15,
62–63
regulation of, 126
for returning privately sponsored
students, 41
by work units, 60
Job mobility
facilitation of, 60–61, 69
of returning graduates, 15
work unit opposition to, 60

L

Li Peng, 30, 32, 38, 118
Liu Zhongde, 29–30, 31
Lu Jiaxi, 60

M

Ministry of Education, 24, 25–27; *see
also* State Education
Commission
Modernization of China
through academic exchanges,
22–23, 115
employment problems, 58–59,
61–65
housing problems, 65
incentives for productivity
increases, 48
normalization of relations with
U.S., 21
obstacles to, 19–20, 60

N

National Conference on Study
Abroad, 29
National Defense Science,
Technology, and Industry
Commission, 62

O

Officially sponsored
students/scholars
contracts/agreements with work
units, 30, 73, 129
definition, 6–7
detail required in visa applications,
85
fellowship limits, 31
financing by host universities, 31
number, 9–10, 119
passport source, 78
preparation and training, 130
return of, 4, 13
selection criteria, 129
state program personnel, 127
statistics on, 78, 80
unit program personnel, 127
women, 96

P

PhDs, Chinese
distribution by field, 102–103
foreign-trained, 115

funding for exchanges with foreign experts, 31
home-trained, 13, 37
temporary workplaces for, 69–70
wages of, 64
Policy of opening to outside world
channels of knowledge created by, 22–23
Confucian traditions and, 20
emigration of students and, 120
evolution of, 19–35
historical background, 19–22
see also Modernization of China
Privately sponsored students/scholars
characteristics of, 42, 98–100
discrimination against returning students, 41
emigration/delayed returns, 4, 14, 36–37, 113
fields of study, 11
number, 9, 88, 112
passport source, 78
policy on foreign study by, 31, 40, 135–137
sponsorship by U.S. relatives, 40, 92
tracking of, 81
see also Self-supporting students; Visas/visa holders, F-1
Production-related research, shortages of, 72

R

Regulation of foreign study
administrative requirements, 125–126
age limits, 106, 128
agreements/contracts with work units, 30, 73
Embassy/Consular oversight of students, 8, 50, 126
expense management, 130–132
fields of study, 124–125, 131
financing by work unit, 29, 125
foreign language requirements, 128
home leave, 133–134
implementation problems, 14, 27, 33–35, 50, 120–121
job arrangements for returnees, 126

joint Chinese/U.S. degree programs, 51–52
liberalization of, 27–28
limits on length of study, 50, 118, 127
political qualifications of students, 127–128
postdoctoral research/practical training, 131–133
for privately sponsored students, 40, 41, 135–137
quotas by field of study, 73
rumors about, 32–33
selection process, 26, 27–28, 30, 38, 49–50, 118–119, 126–131, 132
seniority of returnees, 130
spouse visitation, 134–135
state sponsored versus privately sponsored students, 34
State Education Commission provisions on study abroad, 123–137
U.S. changes to facilitate, 120–121
visiting scholars, 106
vocational qualifications of students/scholars, 128
wages, 130, 132
work requirement before going abroad, 30–31, 34, 40, 50, 133
Research facilities and equipment
complaints of domestic graduates about, 66
complaints of foreign-trained scholars about, 63–64, 65, 66–67, 102, 116
misuse of funds for, 64
open research laboratories, 69–70
proposed improvements in, 69
temporary holding centers and research opportunities, 69–70
Research/visiting scholars
age limit, 106
attitudes about production research, 116
definition, 7
expense management, 133
funding of, 108
J-1 visa holders, statistics on, 106–109
number, 24
regulation of, 131–133

selection process, 132
specializations, 108–109, 132–133
women, 106–107
work requirement for, 133
Returning students/scholars
administrative duties, 68
basic research opportunities, 117
characteristics of, 8, 62, 64, 65, 96
choice of employment, 59
complaints of, 14–15, 41, 58, 59,
    62–68, 102, 116
discrimination against, 41, 63, 66
estimation of, 111
expectations by, 62, 64
expectations of, 67–68
historical role of, 19
inducements for, 5, 9, 14, 29, 31,
    41, 43–44, 49–52, 54–55, 68–73,
    96, 117
information availability on, 81
job mobility, 15
legitimacy of complaints, 65–68
linkages with foreign counterparts,
    68
misuse/misassignment of, 14–15,
    59, 62–63, 65, 66
number of, 13, 27, 43, 113
preferential treatment of, 28–29,
    61–62
research fellowships for, 69
solutions to problems of, 68–73
tension between domestic
    graduates and, 58
tracking problems, 83–84, 85
utilization of, 27, 57–73
wages, 64–65, 67, 68, 116
work requirements before returning
    abroad, 30–31
working conditions, 63

S

Scholastic Aptitude Tests, 25
Scientific and Technological Associ-
    ation of Hunan Province, 65
Self-supporting students/scholars;
    definition, 7; *see also* Privately
    sponsored students/scholars
Sino-Soviet academic exchanges, 20
State Education Commission, 24, 29,
    32, 37, 38, 51–52, 58, 71, 73, 78,
    81, 119, 123–137

Statistics on Chinese students
Chinese statistics, 77–81, 101
F-1 visa holders, 39, 88–105
fields of study, 100–104
financial support sources, 94–95
J-1 visa holders, 39, 88–109
personal characteristics, 95–100
problems with, 77–86
students and scholars, 88–93
students only, 94–106
U.S. Immigration and
    Naturalization Service, 39,
    82–84
from U.S. Information Agency data
    tapes, 85–86, 94, 100
from visa applications, 84–85, 94,
    100, 110
visiting scholars, 106–109
Student demonstrations
academic exchanges, effect on, 1–2,
    31–32, 120
official reaction to, 3, 47
reactions of students abroad to,
    4–5, 13–14, 120
see also Intellectual dissent
Students, *see* Chinese students
    abroad

T

Taiwanese students
complaints of, 66
statistics on number in U.S., 82, 83
Talent Exchange and Consultation
    Service Centers, 60
Technology transfer
through acquisition of plant and
    equipment packages, 72
in practical training of scholars, 51
Test of English as a Foreign
    Language, 24–25, 28–29

U

Understanding of Educational
    Exchanges, 23
United Nations Institute for
    Training and Research, studies
    of brain drain issue, 53–54
Universities, Chinese
enrollments of graduate students,
    37

fields of study, 71
foreign students in, 81
improvements in, 13, 37
Jiaotung, 62
joint degree programs with U.S.
  universities, 51–52
limitations on slots, 40–41, 93, 104
Qinghua, 62
University of Science and
  Technology, 62
women in, 96
Universities, U.S.
  funding of Chinese students/
    scholars, 31, 90–91, 108, 115
  preferences of Chinese students,
    104–106
  value of Chinese students to,
    117–118
  waiver of standardized tests for
    Chinese students, 24–25
U.S. Dept. of State, Visa Office,
  statistics on Chinese students in
  U.S., 82–83, 100, 110
U.S. Immigration and Naturalization
  Service
  policy on deportation, 5, 8–9, 49,
    84, 117
  statistics of Chinese students, 39,
    82–84
U.S. Information Agency,
  information on Chinese students
  in U.S., 84–86, 94–95, 100

V

Visas/visa holders, F-1
  characteristics of students/scholars,
    84, 96
  Consulate-issued versus
    Embassy-issued, 88–90
  definition, 6
  educational background, 98–100
  emigration/delayed returns of, 4, 9,
    39, 40, 112–113
  estimation of, 112–113
  fields of study, 11, 13, 96, 100–101
  financial support sources, 86
  gender differences in, 96
  geographic distribution in U.S.,
    104–106
  geographic origins of, 92–93
  I-20 form, 6

marital status, 96
number issued, 9–10, 40, 88, 94,
  110
tracking problems, 83, 112
women, 11
Visas/visa holders, F-2
  definition, 6
  number issued, 96
Visas/visa holders, J-1
  characteristics of students/scholars,
    14, 38, 84–85
  computerization of data on, 80–81
  Consulate-issued versus
    Embassy-issued, 88–90
  definition, 6
  emigration of, 39
  extension for practical training, 51
  fields of study, 11–13, 96, 100–102
  financial support sources, 11, 31,
    85, 90–91, 94–95
  gender differences in, 96
  geographic distribution in U.S.,
    104–106
  geographic origins of, 92–93
  IAP-66 form, 6, 38, 84–86, 110
  limits on length of stay, 13
  marital status, 96
  number issued, 9–10, 81, 88,
    110–112
  occupations of, 98–99
  professional standing of, 98–99
  returns to China, 4, 38–39, 111
  statistics on, 81, 85
  tracking problems, 83
  two-year rule, 7, 39
  visiting scholars, 106–109
  women, 11, 107
Visas/visa holders, J-2
  number issued, 96

Y

Yang Wei, 120
Yang Xinguan, 2

Z

Zhang Jingfu, 27, 63–64, 69
Zhao Fusan, 45–46
Zhao Ziyang, 3, 4, 45